My Blasted Town

Town

ADVENTURES OF A MISFIT

DANIEL J. MILLETTE

Copyright © MMXXIII
Saskatchewan, Canada
Launch Publishing

My Blasted Town

Adventures of a Misfit

Editing by Shavonne Clarke
Cover design by Duy Phan

ISBN eBook: 978-1-7780525-6-9
ISBN Paperback: 978-1-7780525-5-2

danieljmillette.substack.com
www.youtube.com/@DanielJMillette
www.facebook.com/DanielJMillette

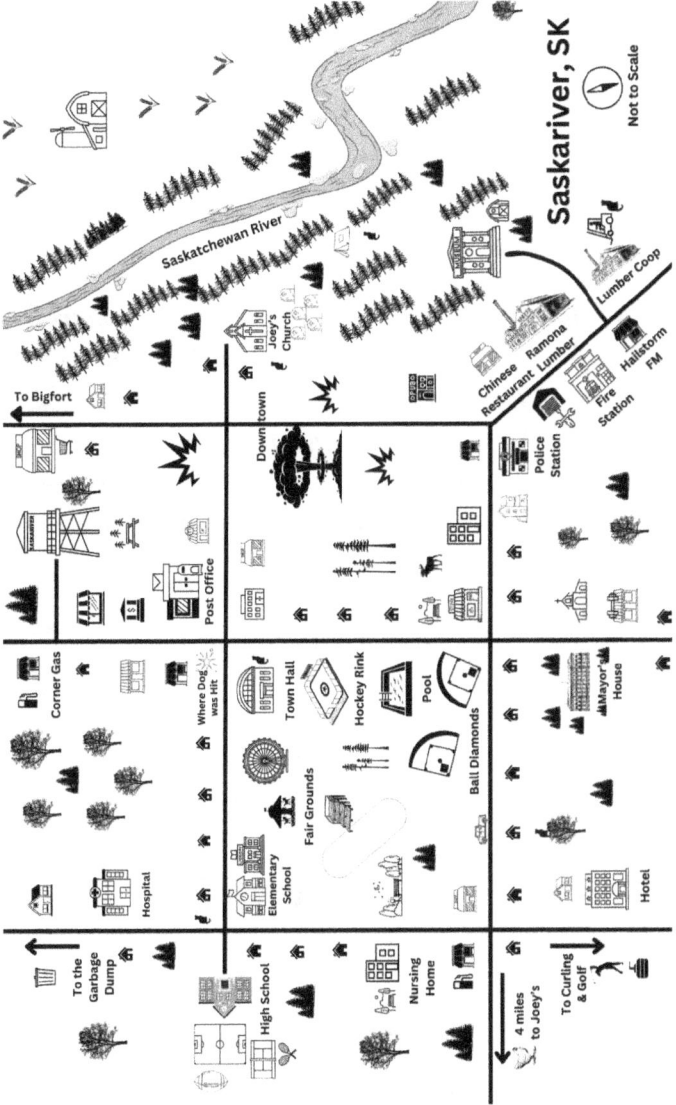

Saskariver, SK

Not to Scale

Saskatchewan River

To Bigfort

Downtown

Joey's Church

Chinese Restaurant

Ramona Lumber

Lumber Coop

Hailstorm FM

Police Station

Fire Station

Post Office

Corner Gas

Where Dog was Hit

Town Hall

Hockey Rink

Pool

Ball Diamonds

Mayor's House

Fair Grounds

Hospital

Elementary School

Hotel

To the Garbage Dump

High School

Nursing Home

4 miles to Joey's

To Curling & Golf

DISCLAIMER

*T*his book is a work of fiction. Characters are fictional. Events are fictional. Saskariver is fictional. The author does not have time for petty fictional assertions claiming otherwise.

Having said all that, there is one name that is real. Jennie. I have enclosed a brief story about her at the end of this book.

DEDICATION

To the author who has impressed, influenced, and inspired me more than words could ever express:

Wendell Berry.

For me, Port William is more magical than Narnia.

A THOUGHT

"There are moments when the heart is generous, and then it knows that for better or worse our lives are woven together here, one with one another and with the place and all the living things."

—— Wendell Berry, *Jayber Crow*

Chapter One

The Graveyard

I'm half sure I'm dead right now. *At least* half sure. Only two things keep me from 100% certainty. First, I've got a sharp pain in my left arm from the fall. I'd thought, or hoped, that death would remove all pain. That there would be no sting. But no dead person ever warned me what to expect. And second, I haven't seen Jesus anywhere. Not yet. Maybe Jesus is taking his time getting to me. How long should I wait?

No, I must be dead. At first, there were stars in my mind when I fell. Like sparks of electricity piercing an endless night. Now, there is just this endless night. All darkness. My world has collapsed. I am already in the grave. It is cold, hard, and creepy. Not a pleasant way to go. The Egyptians had the right idea by burying their dead with all their stuff. I could use my dog Doggy right now. I would even be sort of happy with one of my cats.

Did I mention it is dark? Dark, lonely, and getting colder. Rest in peace, Joey Storthoaks. At the ripe old age of eleven. Only the sort-of-good die young.

What brought me to this place? What am I doing *here*? That is my story, and seeing as Jesus might be a little late in coming to get me, I don't mind sharing it.

I must admit I've been here before. And where is that? The Saskariver Cemetery. It's near the river's edge, surrounded by evergreen forest and willow bush. Deer, moose, and bears make their way to the cemetery. Skunks, cougars, and coyotes too. It's a regular meeting place. I never feared such critters here, though. I feared much worse.

In the woods behind the Saskariver Cemetery lives a man. One might call him homeless, but that would be incorrect. He lives out in the bush behind the graves because he *chooses* to do so. It is his home. As with the bears, cougars, and coyotes, this man wants to be close to the graves. The constant presence of death is his comfort.

I'm told that this man buries his victims behind the cemetery—that the animals come to receive scraps of...food from him. I'm told he's always looking for his next victim, that even the police are scared of him, that he even once made a victim out of a policeman. I'm told he once lost a child in an accident and that it messed with his head. I'm told he has a patch over one eye because the covered eye is a demon's.

I'm told these things because I live in a small town in Saskatchewan, Canada. Every small town has a story like this. And it is a right of passage for every young person to investigate it. To go *there*. To live, to tell. If not to live, then to decrease the surplus population. I did just that one day. I did go *there*, with my older brother Josh and our friend Xander Humboldt. I am younger than both of them by three years. I suppose that put me in a difficult spot. The youngest must always do the dirty work. One of these days I'll make my younger brother Sam do the same. If I get back to life.

❧ 🦌 ❧

It was early May, and the leaves hadn't quite filled the trees yet. We were at church that Friday evening. There was a youth group retreat of sorts. It was either attending the youth group or cleaning the chicken coop at home. I should've stayed home and cleaned the chicken coop. Chickens don't try to lay hands on you to heal you.

Inside the church, there was some form of music to occupy our time. You know the songs where the boys sing the first part, the girls sing the second, then all join together on the final go-around? Imagine boys having to rhyme words like *fire* and *desire* while singing next to a group of girls. "You light my fire... My heart's desire..." It's meant for God, I think. But I swear some of those girls take it in other ways. They blush and glow. Some of the boys like that. Not me. Well, on that one night, the songs became giggle-fests. The youth group leaders threatened to "lay hands" over us in prayer to have us smarten up.

We smartened up just in time for the testimonial section. Teenagers were crying over how they had found Jesus. These teenagers were the same ones who swore and smoked behind the school just hours earlier. But I'm sounding bitter. I'm just jealous that I still have yet to find Jesus here in my grave.

The church retreat was getting emotional. Josh and Xander did the only sensible thing they could and snuck out into the cool spring evening. I would've left with a friend my age, but I don't have any friends worth mentioning. Friendship isn't my strong suit. So, I snuck out with Josh and Xander. We made our way to the nearby cemetery. Darkness was settling in, where just enough light was available to see what was ahead of you. A vague, shadowy vision. Like a horror movie.

"What are we doing?" I asked Xander and Josh.

"Shut up and keep quiet!" yelled Xander, unaware of the irony of his words. "You're the slowest here, aren't you? We can leave you behind alone if we want, dead or alive," he threatened. Thirty minutes earlier, Xander had been testifying at the retreat that he was a perfectly saved young man.

I followed the boys right through the graveyard. We were heading west towards the bush near the river. A tombstone reached out and tripped me. I stumbled forward, right into Josh's backside. He tumbled over onto Xander, who in turn knocked over a solar lantern placed near an old grave where the words "Rest in Peace" shouted a warning at us.

Feeling somehow responsible for my mess-up, my brother amended the situation, knocking me flat on my back and hissing, "If you get us killed, then I'll kill you!" I knew he meant it, too.

We made our way to the cemetery's edge and shimmied through branches and trees toward the last glimpses of light. The rose bushes scraped at my cheeks as we passed through, but I didn't make a sound.

"Shh, you brat!" shouted Xander, again unaware of himself. "I think I see something through the bush."

"Is that a blue tarp?" asked Josh, peering through the remaining cover of branches and trees.

My heart pounded through my chest, into my limbs, and echoed to the rest of the world. Not a blue tarp! Anything but a blue tarp.

"It's set up like a tent," added Xander. "Someone *does* live here. It's true. It's real." He turned towards us and said, "It's gonna kill us."

My brother Josh did the only thing he knew possible at that dreadful moment. With his voice shaking like the pelvis of Elvis, he offered a great sacrifice for the good of all. That is, he sacrificed his own brother.

"Joey, go check it out," he said. "We'll watch from here to see if anyone comes."

"I'm not..."

"Get going! Or else I'll tell Mom who's been sneaking the chips at night."

Checkmate. That was worse than his threat to kill me. I knew I was done. I took a step forward. The air was thick with tension. Another step. A chill ran through my bones. Two more steps. Before I knew it, I was standing in a small clearing, maybe thirty feet in diameter. There indeed was a blue tarp set up like a tent. I saw rusty cans and old bottles. A makeshift fireplace was in the middle of it all. And a small table. It was probably an altar of sacrifice where cats and eleven-year-old children were offered.

"Hurry up!" bellowed Xander from the bush, with his usual lack of self-awareness.

Unsure of what I was supposed to do, I panicked and bent to pick up an old bottle to bring back with me. Sort of a souvenir to prove my courage. Like that hobbit did once in the dragon's lair. But it was getting dark, and as I reached to pick up what I thought was a dark wine bottle, instead, my hand clutched something soft and warm. The warm blob exploded at the touch, jumped three feet in the air, and screeched a murderous yell.

"Scram!" shouted Xander.

It was every man for himself. I jumped out of my skin, nearly out of my soul, and dove into the bush. The cat I had evidently disturbed fled in front of me. I unknowingly stepped on its tail this time as I scrambled for cover. That darn cat. We both went sprawling. My face landed on the edge of one of those rose bushes, the kind where even the tiniest of pricks makes you want to cry like a baby, and I crawled on all fours into those thorns in front of me. Just as my backside was covered and I was near passing out with a half-inch thorn in my chin, I heard a grizzly man's voice from the bush on the other side of the clearing.

"I'm coming for you!"

Off like a shot. Through the bush, through thorns and willows, and into the cemetery. Xander and Josh were already gone from sight. Possibly they were back in the church by now, claiming to be saved. Not me. I was still halfway through the cemetery. No man's land. Death literally all around. I needed saving, alright.

A crackle sounded from the trees behind me. What to do? As I ran, I saw a piece of plywood on the ground next to a mound of dirt. The plywood was covering a large hole. The hole was undoubtedly made to welcome a dead body in the next day or two. I had two choices: go in this hole, temporarily, or be caught by the creep and end up in one of his holes, permanently. It was no choice at all. I stopped at the edge of this fresh hole, breathed, and jumped in.

It's true. They do dig graves six feet down. And it's also true, a six-foot hole is deep. A-foot-over-my-brown-hair deep. What on earth was I thinking? I was trapped. Unable to shout for help for fear of attracting the local killer. Unable to move. This was my first experience of life in the grave. Not to be my last.

CHAPTER TWO

CATS AND COOPS

That was the first time I was in the grave. Getting out was easy then.

But I'm in the grave again, dead or alive, and it looks like I'm not getting out. So, I have time to tell the whole story. It's a story of my family, my town, my future, my lack of a future. It's a story of foolish bravery and brave foolishness. Of being a misfit. On being misunderstood. On being accepted. It's my story.

There is much to say. There are crazy events to describe. Fire, destruction, parades, and a cake-loving celebrity who happens to be a moose. But first, context. Give me a minute. I need to explain who I am, who I live with, and where I live. Don't worry, I'm not too dull.

🍁 🫎 🍁

I live on an acreage near Saskariver, Saskatchewan, where the prairie meets the northern forest. We have a horse named Horse, a dog named Doggy, two dozen chickens named Breakfast, Dinner, Supper, and so forth, and an unknown number of cats called everything from Cat to

Catsputin, from Kitty to Kitty-Cat, from Poopsy-Diaper to Terrence Pickles. Creativity is a must when you name so many cats over the years. We used to name our cats after politicians, but Mom said it was inappropriate for us to be so happy whenever a cat died.

I also have family members. Not as many as I have cats, but still quite a few, and with less creative names. We all have brownish hair, blue or green eyes, and French-Canadian blood running in our veins. My dad Marc and mom Geri lead the way, followed by Johnny (17), Josh (14), Ellie (13), me (I'm Joey, age 11), Rebecca (6), Sam (4), and the baby Lyda. We get along very well sometimes. Sometimes, we get put to work because we're fighting. Sometimes, we then start fighting while we work. Sometimes, we miss supper until we start being nice to each other. And then we're back where we started.

*　🦌　*

Siblings are funny things. They can be mean and nasty, but in the end, they'll always be there for you. Like when I told you I jumped into the six-foot grave to escape the crazy man by the cemetery. In the end, my brother Josh came back for me and even helped me out of my hole. When I stepped out, he socked me with a right cross, nearly knocking me back in. Brotherly love. But he still saved me, and that counts for something. I think life would be boring without siblings. Cats cannot keep you occupied like a potato-throwing fight with brothers and sisters can.

Life is simple where we live. Chores keep us busy. Sports keep us interested. Food keeps us happy. When something is broken, we fix it. When something is not broken, we usually break it. When we are broke from breaking so many things, we fix ways to make money. Some say that a simple life is boring. I believe every day is a new adventure. It isn't boring if you have the patience to see it. Let me explain...

One day, our chicken coop needed repairs. It started when a mysterious flying potato went through a window. Thankfully, the chickens ate the potato evidence. With the window broken, my dad was finally convinced to repair the cage wiring, roof, walls, and door. Basically, we needed to build a new chicken coop, though my dad would never admit that's what we were doing (because it was originally my mom's idea, I suppose). "The floor's good!" he boasted. It was a lovely floor, when not covered in chicken poop.

Off to town we went on a Saturday morning. It was the day after my rescue from the grave. Feeling free and thankful to be alive, while also noting the chores needing attention around the house, I asked my dad if I could tag along. He agreed. We hopped into his old orange truck and headed to the lumberyard for supplies.

The Lumber Coop. A place where people and stories meet. The smell of year-old spruce, sappy pine, and burning diesel brings a warm welcome to the wearied builder.

The wood is twisted yet charming. Just like the workers there. They are beacons of friendliness and care. Mostly.

"What the heck do you want?" spluttered the short man behind the lumber counter. Ron Spitballer was on his name tag.

"Yeah, eh. We need some stuff for our chicken coop," said my dad.

"You came to the right place," said Ron. His face was stern—his voice sharp. "This *is* the Lumber Coop."

A full ten seconds passed. Statistically speaking, forty-five babies were born in the world during the pause. Another twenty people died. Yet still we stood and stared at Ron, his dark eyes unflinching as they stared back at us.

"Lumber...*Coop*," Ron finally added with great emphasis. The corner of his lip gave a slight twitch. Then he gave one short laugh. It sounded halfway between a clearing of the throat and a raven shouting that it had found roadkill.

I don't know why, but I laughed at his laugh. It just seemed the right thing to do. It broke the ice. It also gave Ron wind under his sails. Which in fact made it the wrong thing to do.

He continued, "Eggcellent! What stuff can we pluck for you? Some im-peck-able lumber? Order before ten o'cluck and I'll give you a deal. Hehe. I should be a comedi-hen."

Ten more seconds passed. More births. More deaths. This time, my dad nudged my head with his elbow, and I bit my tongue to keep from smirking. Best not to encourage him.

Free eggs every morning sure are expensive. That is, we ordered our supplies. Lumber, shingles, nails, wire, windows, a door, and even a little metal sign that said, *Warn-*

ing: Fowl Language Inside. That was Ron Spitballer's idea. When finished, Ron pulled out a walkie-talkie-style radio and barked, "Yard clerk to the shingles! Hey? Are any of you sawed-off little runts out there? I said I need a yard clerk! You little punks! Answer my calls, or you're all fired! Answer! Or I'll come to your homes and pee in your gardens."

No answer came. Ron said to go out to the yard, and someone would help, even if he had to handcuff a worker himself and drag the worker's dead corpse by a forklift to assist us. So, Dad and I stepped out the door into the magical world of the back lumberyard. Dad handed me the yellow order paper and went to the parking lot to get our truck. I stood alone, waiting. Just then, a forklift whizzed by. I held out my order paper for the worker to see.

"No way!" yelled the driver with dark glasses. He was in a hurry. "I've got twenty hours of work to do in five minutes! I'm too busy!" His voice trailed as he steered violently around a turn and towards a back warehouse.

More workers passed by. One waved and said he'd be there as soon as his coffee break was over. Another smiled and said he had to see Ron and book his vacation time first. And still, I stood. Alone. Waiting for help.

The distinct sound of a meow caught my attention. I turned and saw a lumberyard worker strolling towards me. He had *friendly* written all over him. Possibly because of his massive smile and kind eyes. Possibly because he was petting a cat in his arms as he approached. Definitely because he had the time of day to help me.

"Uh, my dad and I need some help," I stated.

"Yeah. Yeah. Don't we all need help?" he laughed, his voice sounding like a slightly cracked trumpet. His chin jiggled.

I held out our paper, and he read it while stroking the cat. The cat purred. He continued, "Ahh shoot. Yeah. That's a lot of stuff. Yeah. I got my hands full here. And everyone else is too lazy. Yeah. But we'll see what we can do. We'll need the forklift to get a stack of lumber down from the shelf. Aw yeah."

I wanted to offer to hold the cat, but the man spoke up first. "I can't put this cat down. It might run off. Belongs to somebody. Or they belong to it. Yeah. There's the darn forklift over there. Just hop into it and drive it around to the back. Yeah."

"But...I can't drive a forklift!"

"Yeah. Just...put your seatbelt on, maybe," he replied. "That should make it okay. Yeah. By the way, they call me Mustache." His clean-shaven face smiled warmly as he held out the cat's paw to be shaken.

"I'm Joey," I said. "We need to fix our chicken coop."

"Eggcellent!" said Mustache. Not this again.

I hopped into the forklift, stepped on the clutch, and turned the key. What-do-ya-know? Diesel exhaust kicked out into the warm blue air. The thing started. After a few tense words and curses from Mustache, I was able to maneuver the forklift to where it needed to be and even pull down the lumber lift.

Thankfully, I stepped out of the forklift just before my dad arrived. There's not much else to say. We loaded up all the supplies into our truck. By we, I mean Dad and I.

Mustache pointed out what needed to be done and where the best wood in the pile was located.

"Yeah. You gotta get the good stuff," he boomed while petting the sleeping cat. "Lazy people I work with. I gotta do everything. Aw yeah."

My dad and I arrived home, and the work began. Most of my siblings came out, and we organized our day. Wood here. Windows there. Wire stacked aside. Kick curious cats away. Radio on. Tools out.

Just then, my mom called from the house. "There's a man at the Lumber Coop on the phone! Says we might've lost a cat when we were there today?"

I looked at my dad, and he looked at me. I will not repeat the words he said then. My mom and I were soon in our family vehicle, driving the four miles into town. We arrived to see Mustache standing out front. He was stroking a different cat in his arms this time. Sure enough, it was one of ours.

"Fluffy!" I shouted at the scruffy, half-beaten tomcat in Mustache's arms. "Dad says he must've traveled in the wheel well," I explained.

"Yeah. Cats do that. Goodbye, Fluffy!" he trumpeted.

Mom and I drove home, and I went back to work. All the walls of the old chicken coop were down, and one new one was now standing in its place, braced by a 2x4 piece of lumber. Meanwhile, there were chickens everywhere, clucking in amusement.

We were ready to hoist up a second wall when Mom called from the house again. "Hey! The Lumber Coop is on the phone again. They said we might have another cat there!"

I learned a few new words from Dad at this latest announcement. My dad sent my oldest brother Johnny and me to town this time. But first, Dad checked all the wheel wells before letting us go.

Once again, we met Mustache out front of the Lumber Coop. Sure enough, he was holding a different cat. It was our precious little momma cat named Mr. T. Checking the gender of a cat was never our strong suit.

"Don't worry, Mustache," I said confidently, "we checked the wheel wells this time. No more cats."

"Yeah. That's fine. I don't mind. Forces the other workers here to do something for a change. Yeah."

Back home we went. All four walls were up, and Dad was busy building trusses for the roof. They fit perfectly, and Dad was happy. Then the Lumber Coop called again, and Dad was not happy.

Back to town. We checked the engine area, all four wheel wells, and both bumpers this time. We came back with our teenage cat Farty Marty.

The roof was on, and the shingling had begun. Ellie and I laid out the shingles while Dad and my brothers hammered the nails. Then Dad and I started installing a door and windows while my other siblings rolled out the new chicken wire. As Dad was about to swing his hammer to install a window, my mom called out again with the old familiar news.

Smash! went the new window as Dad's hammer missed the mark. A flood of new words arose. This was not a safe place for a cat to be at that moment.

"Tell that Mustache guy he can keep the cat. He can keep all of them," shouted Dad.

"No!" protested Ellie. "If we don't get the cats, Grandpa says we'll have mice everywhere! And anyway, they're my little cutie-baby-pies."

Dad stared ahead while contemplating these words. His green eyes were darkening with confused anger—a dozen cats lazed in the sunshine. One of them wheezed up a piece of grass. Another spooked and darted for the bush when a small butterfly landed near it.

Dad's lips curled up, and he pronounced, "Geri, tell Mustache to bring the cat here with their Lumber Coop truck. And while he's at it, have him bring another window."

That settled it. No more cat adventures. It was time to finish the job. We got the shingling done and were ready to tackle the chicken wire. But our work was interrupted again—this time by incessant honking. A large red-and-white, three-ton truck turned into our yard. At the wheel was Mustache. More precisely, a precious little kitten was at the wheel, Mustache sitting behind the adorable little thing.

Oh, it was the cutest little cat I've ever seen. I could see its shining green eyes sparkle from where I stood. It was, as my sister would say, purrfect.

Mustache pretended to have the kitty give two more honks of the truck's horn. From the house, my mom's voice rang in reply, "I just got the baby to sleep!"

Mustache directed us to where the window was stored, and we unloaded it for him. He informed us that he had waited twenty minutes to find another worker to load it for him at the lumberyard—"those lazy workers there. Yeah."

Then it was time to break the news to Mustache. I spoke up on behalf of the Storthoaks family: "Uh...I don't think that cat is ours. Not this time."

A lump was building in my throat. The kitty wiggled its nose at me as if on cue, and I nearly melted on the spot. Doggy came over to smell it. Instantly, the cat purred affection. It was all so right. Like the heavens opened up and a voice from on high declared it good—very good.

"No problem! Yeah. I'll just drive around until I find out who owns it. I've done all the work at the lumberyard today anyway," said Mustache. He hopped into the massive truck with the kitty still in his arms, gave two more loud honks, and drove away. The baby in the house started crying. It wasn't meant to be.

For the rest of the day, we worked without interruption. In the end, we had a small chicken coop ready for business. I nailed my *Fowl Language* sign into place, and we stepped back to admire our work. While I was looking, another cat ran up to my leg and started rubbing its head against us.

"Hey, isn't that Tony Skaponi?" shouted my younger sister Rebecca.

"She's back!" hollered Ellie.

"Hasn't been here in a month or more!" I added.

"Thank goodness. There were mice everywhere without her," said my dad, rolling his eyes.

Just then, as the late-afternoon sun beamed gloriously on me, on us, on this place on Earth, it occurred to me. A hope arose. More than that, an expectation. One of completeness. I ran into the house to make a phone call.

We were all inside around the table an hour later, eating an early supper. Mom was dishing out some potatoes for my younger brother Sam when we heard a familiar honk from the driveway. Our baby started crying from the bedroom.

"Just one more time," began Mom, "and I swear I'll..."

"It's okay, Mom!" I yelled, jumping from my chair. Everyone else followed me out the front door. Well, Mom went to the bedroom to get little Lyda.

Mustache was stepping out of the three-ton truck. He had that same glorious, bright-eyed kitty in his left arm and an apple in his right hand. Those two were sharing the apple. Mustache was tense as he held the kitty. Like his world was about to be shattered.

And it was. At that precise moment, Tony Skaponi wandered between Mustache and the rest of us. She gave a meow, which, in cat language, translates to: "Get the heck over here."

The kitty jumped from Mustache's arms and ran to Tony Skaponi. It was an instant reunion.

"Oh no! Yeah," said Mustache in sorrow. He composed himself, adding, "I guess she's with her momma now."

"Tony Skaponi was pregnant, then she went missing," I explained. "We thought that was the end. But when she showed up today, I knew what had happened. She'd caught a ride to town once, had her kitten at the lumberyard, and stayed there. She probably survived on mice."

"What a mouser!" interrupted Ellie.

"Anyway," I continued, "when I saw Tony Skaponi today, I could tell she was this cute kitty's momma. They have the same eyes."

"Mesmerizing eyes, yeah," said Mustache.

"They're reunited now," said Dad. "A perfect day."

"You mean purrfect, right? Yeah," boomed Mustache. Then he got quiet. He stared at the little kitten on the ground next to its mother. It bounced and played while the momma licked its fur. All was well. It's funny how painful a good thing can be.

"G...g...goodbye, little fella," said Mustache, his voice choking.

He turned back to his truck, desperate to hide tears in his eyes. I bent down and picked up the little kitten. Its eyes were so bright. Its face was a pure, clean-shaven white. And then I announced what seemed only fitting: "Hey, fella, I name you Little Mustache."

Mustache, the human, turned his face and, with a tear rolling down his cheek, beamed a smile the size of the three-ton truck. His life seemed near complete.

My mom stepped out of the house, holding little Lyda in her arms. "Would you care to have some supper with us? Or do you have to go back to work right away? We're having chicken."

Mustache's eyes lit up. "Oh, I don't need to be back for a half hour or so. I could probably stay and eat a bit. Maybe hold Little Mustache, too."

He carefully took Little Mustache out of my arms and stroked him, or her, a few times. Little Mustache purred contentedly.

"Yeah. It's about time those other guys at the lumber-yard do some work anyway. Yeah."

LITTLE MUSTACHE

CHAPTER THREE

MY TOWN JUST BLEW UP

I hope you get some idea of my life, my family, and my town. But I guess I should get back to the main story. Why am I in this grave? You'd better sit down as I tell you what happened. It's serious. You might even say it's grave.

❦ 🫎 ❦

A sunny spring Friday. It was a beautiful morning. Or afternoon. Details get foggy. I was in town with my mom and three younger siblings. Saskariver has about 4,000 people, or so its residents claim. No one really checks. My three older siblings were at school. Real school. Us younger ones homeschool. Don't ask. We were on the way to the post office. This is an exciting outing if you're homeschooled. It gets you out into the real world. You get to see people—actual people—and pretend like you belong among them. They usually stare at you and ask, "Why aren't you in school?"

I walked out of our large family vehicle towards the post office doors. I remember hearing a squirrel chirping across the street and a dog barking at it. My younger brother Sam stood beside me. The wind swayed the branches of trees with gentle ease. The warmth of the day felt good after the long winter. It was all so pleasant. Like nothing could ever go wrong. I need to stop thinking that.

Mom and the other kids stayed in the vehicle while Sam and I walked the steps to the main entrance. Typically we would run around the wheelchair ramp, but this day I was too excited to waste time. As we approached, two old men were standing next to the doors chatting, as old men do.

"Sure could use more rain," said the taller one with the hat floating almost in thin air above his bald head.

"Eh?" came the smaller, rounder, other man wearing a hat so low it covered most of his face. "Who's in pain, you say?"

"What'd you say?"

"Hey?"

"Well, I guess I should go check to see if my name is on the board," chuckled the taller man, fulfilling his daily duty of making this same joke. The board is where all death notices are posted inside the building.

"You named your gourd?" commented the other.

"What about my Ford?"

"Hey?"

"What'd you say?"

I was about to walk past them. Maybe two more steps to climb. I felt a buzzing with anticipation. I was expecting something. A beautiful package, ordered months prior. Another step towards the glass door, and then it hit.

Ker...POW!

Followed by:

BOOM! POW! CRASH! BOOM!

And then, for good measure:

ROAR! Hiss. POW! POW!

It was all in an instant, but it seemed an eternity if that makes any sense. Some force of wind and power shoved me forward. I grabbed my brother as we flew into the shorter man's feet at the door. He nearly stumbled on top of us. It's a good thing he didn't, or we'd be crushed like an elf with Santa sitting on top. The post office door cracked, and a chunk of its glass crashed. Shards of sharp crystals approached but never struck us. Hunching to the ground, feeling heat and power consume me, I veered my head around just in time to see an orange cloud rise across the street. Majestic and fearful, it rose hundreds of feet in the air. Terrified and awed, I grabbed my young brother close.

The orange rose higher, upwards, to new heights. When it seemed heaven itself was about to be burned, and all the angels would singe their wings, the fierce flames mushroomed outward. The mushroom spread wider, expanding in heat and intensity. Farther, ever farther, until it seemed to hit a wall. The orange bomb mercifully faded into the once blue sky, and the rain shower of debris hit.

Bricks, boards, and backhoe pieces raced through the sky, seeking to destroy the earth below. An entire scoop bucket from an excavator fell in the middle of the street, right behind our vehicle. A chunk of lumber went sailing through the window of a nearby video game store. A lady walking her dog stood beside the gaming store. She was frozen with fear. A clump of bricks echoed down from above. A hundred miles an hour, they raced. The target was sickening. I saw the bricks smack her dog on the head right in front of her. Through the roar and chaos, I swear

I heard the *thud* from that impact. The dog crumpled. Killed instantly. The lady slipped as she turned to flee, got up, and slipped again before hiding behind a poplar tree. At that moment, I knew this vision of the dog would be with me as long as I lived.

For forty years, it seemed, the world rained down destruction upon Saskariver. I witnessed it all. *Thud* here. *Smash* there. Vehicle sirens began shrilling, letting the world know something was wrong. Shouts and more minor explosions, too. Dust and smoke raced forward like the angel of death. At one point, a giant sign from the hardware store left its perch and plunged to the sidewalk. Light bulbs shattered. It sounded like firearms discharging a unison of bullets at a shooting range. Only this situation was far deadlier. We were the targets.

Still, I clung to my brother. He was squirming in discomfort, wailing the cry of a four-year-old stuck in a surreal nightmare. Just like that, I felt like a parent protecting my young. I was a man now. Looking up, I saw more flames and smoke, and my body started shaking. I was no longer a man. In my trembling, I felt strong arms cover me. Both old men at the step were stooped down. Their arms were spread out over the top of us, shielding Sam and me with their very lives. It seemed so natural a thing for them to do. The old protecting the young. It was so natural that I never did thank them. They were risking their lives to save us. Death was very possible.

Death. How? How much? How could anyone survive *this*? I should've been thinking these thoughts. Yet I am eleven and not always that aware. These thoughts never entered my mind. I'm not sure what entered my mind.

Nothing reasonable. After the debris stopped falling, I lifted myself from the old men. Ignoring them, I sent my brother back to our vehicle, where my mom's face still held its shocked, panicked look. I turned back to the post office and pulled open the front door. Stepping over shards of glass, I entered the building. I walked, shocked but focused, to our mailbox. I bent down. The key in my hand shook, and I couldn't fit it in the keyhole. Was I shaking, or was the whole building shaking me? I reached with my other hand to steady the key-holding hand. Fumbling about, I somehow inserted the key and gave it a turn. The mailbox door opened; I reached in and pulled out what I wanted.

I came outside just in time to see my mom racing towards me like an angry momma bear. Her look woke me from my daze. Boy, was she mad! Grabbing my arm, she yanked me to our still-intact vehicle. The package in my hand flew from my grip and landed in a bush at the bottom of the steps, where dirt and bricks had rained down just moments ago. She pulled me into the vehicle, where my siblings were crying. And we hunkered down.

For all I could tell, our town had just blown up.

So what actually happened?

A large portion of the main street did blow up. From what I could tell, overhearing my parents talk that night, some workers were digging with heavy equipment behind a local business. They struck a gas pipe. Then—I won't swear because my mom would kill me—all *heck* broke loose. Several stores and shops blew up. I'm not sure how many. Five or six. Others were damaged. A roof here. A front door there. The post office was close, but thankfully, not close enough. Plus, it is an old building and, as my dad would say, *built right.*

"How many people died?" asked my mom.

"That's just it," said Dad. "I heard just a few. Not many. I mean...it's impossible."

"Did they count the dog?" I asked. I was being serious.

"You're lucky you weren't one of them," my mom said, turning to me. "What the heck were you doing going into the post office after it happened?"

"All I know is that there's a perfectly good Lego set sitting in the bush by the post office," I chirped back. That comment earned me an entire evening of vacuuming the house. It was worth it. I think.

"We'll rebuild," said my dad, determined. "The town'll be back. We'll get through this. I'll go with the older boys tomorrow, and we'll help with the cleanup."

The next day, we showed up to help clean the town. One of the emergency workers, sent from a big city, I think—a gruff man who looked stressed, filthy, and unpleasant—took one look at us and told us that they didn't need any large family bugging them. My dad and the guy got into a pretty good argument. But it was all in vain.

"The town'll be back, eh?" I said to Dad as we drove home. He almost left me on the side of the road.

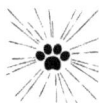

CHAPTER FOUR

TO TOWN

Being homeschooled has distinct advantages and disadvantages. Some think I get to sleep in every morning. I start my school day at 7:30 in the morning and usually finish by noon. Isn't that better? Who wants to be staring at a writing assignment at three o'clock in the afternoon? I love working at my own pace too. Also, I don't miss being bullied at school like I was a few years ago when I went. Okay, I wasn't actually bullied. But I saw others get picked on, and it was sickening. Some kids are sneaky at knowing how to hide bullying from teachers.

However, I think sometimes I have a fear-of-missing-out syndrome. I wonder what others are doing. I imagine what it would be like to go on a field trip with others my age again. The laughter. The friendship. The one kid getting in trouble and having to sit with the teacher. It would differ significantly from our homeschool field trips, where moms run the show. Imagine being on a school bus with diaper changes, Gospel sing-songs, and rambunctious arguments over who is the most courageous character in *The Lord of the Rings*. It's Samwise Gamgee, by the way.

One advantage of being homeschooled is going to town in the middle of the day. It feels like freedom to hear Mom say, "Let's go to town," while knocking on our vehicle hood for an exit of cats. I secretly like it when strangers see me and say, "Why aren't *you* in school?" I usually mutter that I'm homeschooled. But someday, I'd like to say something wittier. Maybe ask the person, "Oh yeah? Why aren't *you* in school?" I need to work on some better comebacks.

I was excited and nervous on that first real visit to town after the explosion. It was about a week after it happened. Rebecca, Sam, Lyda, and I were buckled in and ready. Mom said that the post office was open once again. This meant I could find—or try to find—my lost Lego set. It took many months of allowance to pay for that thing. That shows how small my allowance is.

I will admit that the thought of seeing my hometown blown apart scared me. Apocalyptic movie scenes are cool until they happen in your backyard. What if all that was left was an enormous crater? What if blood stains were on every building? What if visions of that poor dog getting killed flooded my imagination like a vivid, unforgettable nightmare? I could never tell others, but that poor dog's death gave me nightmares twice already. *Thud*. Always that *thud*.

We arrived in town. The familiar advertising sign greeted us: *BOB'S CUSTOM GLASS*. Of course, this is Saskariver. Someone had long ago stolen the *GL* from that last word. I'll let you figure out what it says. Bob just left the sign as-is. It's been there for years. That's the small-town charm for you.

We turned left towards the scene of the action. Soon, the orange brick of the post office shone a familiar glow. I was happy to see it. My happiness soon ended. The post office overlooked a horror scene from a movie. Across the street were blackened-out shops, piles of debris, and even a burned-out backhoe. My little sister Rebecca kept asking, "Mommy, when will they fix it? I don't like this."

We all went into the post office together. As we approached the main doors, sure enough, the same two old men were standing in front. I remembered how they had risked their lives to shield me from the debris asteroids on that fateful explosion day. Probably, I should have thanked them. Or at least smiled. I get shy and nervous at the worst possible time. And then, I get upset with myself later and try and justify what I do or fail to do. I overthink things. Sometimes it's best to act.

After getting the mail, we stepped outside, and I ran down to where my package had fallen. My brother Sam went with me.

"Right here!" I shouted. "Right smack down where I dropped it!"

Sam grabbed the package from my hands to show Mom. I was about to chase after him, but my foot caught a loose brick that had rained from on high days earlier. Down I went, into more bricks and dirt. My left elbow took most of the impact. For the thousandth time, I wondered why they call it a funny bone if it hurts like giving birth four times. Not that I've ever given birth. Or will ever. I'm just assuming that's the degree of pain. My dad says that's pretty close to the pain he has when he has a cold.

The pain of hiding that you're hurt is far worse. I rose to my feet, breathing deeply. Ten seconds. That's all I needed. Looking around, breathing slowly, I noticed where I landed. Maybe eight or ten bricks. Some old scraps of a chocolate bar wrapper. A few splinters of wire. Several buckets of dirt that must've flown hundreds of feet in the air. And an interesting piece of...something.

Walking to the vehicle, I stopped. An interesting piece of...something? Doubling back, I bent over and scooped it up. It was small, and it rested within a quarter-size piece of kimberlite rock—my homeschooling geology unit had some use after all. There was a faint shine to it; the shine part was about half the size of my small fingernail. It was hard. It was mesmerizing. But it couldn't be what I thought it was, could it?

Getting to the vehicle, my mom asked, "What did you find?"

"A nice rock," I answered. Not a complete lie.

"Then throw it out," she said.

"When we get home." I had no intention of throwing it out any time soon.

We had another stop to make: the nearby corner gas station to fill up our vehicle. Clearly, the shiny object was on my mind because I forgot about my Lego set during that time. When I finally looked at the back of the vehicle, Sam had the box and wrappers opened and half the set strewn out over the floor and seats. I could've killed him.

At the gas station, we all jumped out of the vehicle. Along came a pleasant attendant named Danny. Danny was everyone's favorite worker. There were rumors that Danny was an award-winning gas station attendant. Right in our small town! I imagine one day they'll make a giant billboard sign about Danny right next to the *BOB'S CUS-TOM GLASS* one. Needless to say, Danny put on a show.

"Greetings! What a pleasant family. How may I help you?"

"Just fill-er up, please," said my mom.

"Diesel, regular, or premium?"

"Uh, just regular, thanks."

"Would you like your oil checked?"

"No, it's good."

"May I check your windshield wiper fluid level?"

"It's good."

"Brake fluid?"

"Uh, no."

"Power-steering fluid?"

"No."

"Transmission fluid?

"NO."

"Engine coolant?"

"NO!"

"Tire pressure check?"

"NEVER!"

"Wash your windshield?"

"NO THANK YOU!" said my mom, loud enough to be heard across town. She then stomped into the store, though I noted some hesitation. She *did* want the windshield washed. The "no" was a thoughtless mistake. As I entered the gas station building, I looked back at Danny. He saw my look, read my mind perfectly, and then raced a hundred miles an hour to clean our windshield and all other windows, not to mention the headlamps, rear lights, side mirrors, and license plate. What a perfect gas station attendant.

Inside provided a great contrast. While the flawless gas station attendant worked outside, two other workers, about the same age as Danny, "worked" inside. That is, they were playing a floor hockey game using brooms for hockey sticks and a can of chewing tobacco for a puck. One of the boys took a hard slapshot. The chewing tobacco bounced off a stack of chips, knocking them over before nearly hitting me. I dove out of the way, only to land on the chips spilling onto the floor. *Pop!* went a dozen bags of fried potato goodness. I was sprawled on the ground in a mess for the second time in minutes. This time I was surrounded by potato chips crying out to be eaten. Sam and Rebecca came running over to help. So thoughtful.

"Stop eating chips off the floor!" said my mom. We three kids emptied our hands of chips right into our mouths. With Lyda in her arms, Mom bent over and started pulling me out of the mess. "What's this?" she exclaimed with surprise.

"Uh..." I said, and I meant it.

"Is that what you were looking at over by the post office?"

Busted. Mom is my homeschooling teacher. She taught me the geology unit on kimberlite and this other thing. Sigh.

"Joey, if that's what I think it is, we need to hand it over."

"Hand it over? To what, the government?"

"I dunno, the town, I guess. It might be important. We'll stop by the town office on our way home." She said it with that tone of voice that made one believe there would be no arguing. Not if one wanted to live long.

Eventually, we got cleaned enough to pay for the gas and leave. All thanks, of course, to Danny, the wonder-worker who came in, cleaned everyone up, offered a thousand apologies, and even bought us all slushies from his own pocket. What a perfect gas station attendant.

The next stop was to backtrack to the town office. Not a picture-perfect town office, mind you, with stately red brick, a Canadian flag, and a clock tower. Nope. This one had plain tin roofing and siding, an old rusty clock that gave the correct time twice a day, and half a stone monument out front. Rumor was that two town workers had been racing lawnmowers one afternoon ten years ago, and one had crashed into the monument. Maybe it will get fixed in another ten years. They should let Danny run the town. Things would get done. I'd vote for him.

The town office was a busy place. I groaned. We'd be waiting a while! A lineup of at least eight or ten people was waiting to launch lengthy complaints. Probably related to the explosion. As it was, I could hear an older gentleman in a tan jacket and green hat unloading on the front desk worker.

"What do you mean it will take more time for someone to clean up the toilet from my front lawn? I pay taxes! The toilet came from *your* downtown. I pay your salary! I want that toilet gone. I'm a senior!"

The lady at the desk tried to explain that there was a larger mess to clean up downtown. She might as well have tried to convince Buddy the Elf that there is no Santa Claus. What a drag.

"Can we go home, Mom?" I whispered.

"Not until we show them what you found."

Sam, Rebecca, and Lyda began getting restless. Thankfully, I'm an extremely intelligent eleven-year-old—or so I like to think if you ignore my messy hair and ripped sweatpants. Their restlessness gave me an idea. I quietly walked behind Lyda while Mom held her. Just a little pinch on the back of her left leg. No one noticed.

No one except Lyda. She began screaming like she'd been shot—a dramatic little girl. The screams and wails got everyone's attention. Within seconds, three people in line had backed out the main door. A few more shuffled out of the way. Finally, the man at the counter glared back at Lyda. For a few seconds, he stared, unsure whether he could manage the right thing. Finally, he gave way.

"Um, perhaps you'd like to take my place in line. I'm not getting anywhere with these lazy bureaucrats anyway! And I'm a senior! I pay their salaries!"

We took his place. Instantly, Lyda stopped crying. Well played.

"What?" asked the lady at the counter—a real people-pleaser. Danny, the award-winning gas station attendant, would've given us free doughnuts and juice by now if he was in charge.

"My son found something by the post office," said Mom. She held out the object. The lady stared at it, unimpressed. That is until my mom added, "Do you think it could be a diamond? Like something that came from the explosion?"

The lady didn't reply. Her eyes widened. Her dyed black hair seemed to gravitate towards the rock like some magnetic force. Her lips quivered. She called out, "Bob, get Mrs. Nutrine here. Now."

Oh boy. That escalated quickly! Mrs. Nutrine is the mayor. Karen Nutrine. A larger-than-life woman. By that, I mean she is large. Curly-dyed hair. Beady black eyes. Big shrill voice. Kinda scary. Wouldn't you know it, I was about to be famous!

"What, Janet?" bellowed a voice from the back office.

"Come!" said the lady named Janet.

"Darn it! I'm busy working on cleaning these jelly doughnut crumbs from my jacket. Next time get me apple fritters, darn it! I need to look good for those media interviews!"

Eventually, she came out. She didn't even look at us. Just Janet. Then, the kimberlite rock with the mesmerizing insert. Then, a light went on in her mind. And she became an entirely different person.

"Well, now! You found this, young lad? What a charming, brilliant, brave young sir!" Her smooth talk creeped me out. "Look, son," continued Mayor Nutrine, "I think maybe this might belong to someone I know downtown. They will be so happy to hear that you found it."

She reached into a desk drawer behind the counter and fished for something. Then she pulled out two free mini-golf passes. "You deserve this for your great work. If only everyone were as generous as you! Well now, you have a great day."

With that, the mayor turned and left with the rock in her hand. Just like that, I knew it was a diamond. The mayor, I am told, had a background in jewelry. Probably as a robber.

We turned and went home. We had done our civic duty. Our town would be alright, thanks to me. Charming, brilliant, brave young me.

Chapter Five

To Church

A few days later, it was Sunday, the second Sunday since the explosion. However, the church—the entire town—had been shut down immediately after the disaster. So, this was the first Sunday we would be back at church. As we always do, my family raced to make it on time.

There are many reasons we might be late for Mass on Sunday. The older siblings usually sleep in too late. The younger siblings usually lose shoes and clothing at the worst possible time. On the other hand, I am always perfectly prepared, with my hair combed, shirt tucked in, and shoes shined. If you believe that, you'll believe anything. As for my parents, Sunday morning has always been their special time together. My dad spends the first part of the morning reviewing our family finances. At the kitchen table, he and Mom argue about how much money was too much to spend on books, clothes, and chicken coops. *You cannot serve God and money*, sayeth the Good Book. So, they would get the money thing figured out ahead of time.

"Whoa! It says here you spent thirty-four dollars and thirty-eight cents at the Lumber Coop!" my dad might say. "What are you buying there? Groceries made of sawdust?"

"*Maybe* it's for a Father's Day gift!" my mom would reply, though it wasn't actually for a Father's Day gift. "I don't snoop on your Mother's Day gifts. If you ever remember to buy one."

"And what about seventeen dollars and sixty-six cents at the gas station? That can't be gas. Buying snack foods? Or is this a Father's Day gift too?"

And so on. As was the case this morning, it was time to leave the world of money and head to the world of God, late. *Late have I loved you*, I think a wise man once said. The mad rush was on.

"Let's go! Did *everyone* go to the bathroom?"

"Do a headcount!"

"Are we gonna forget the baby again?"

"You can't wear *that* to church?"

"We're only missing one shoe. That ties our record."

"I'm leaving in thirty seconds. I mean it."

"Just honk the horn, and all the kids will come."

The horn honked that morning. Six kids made it to the vehicle (Ellie was holding Lyda). That's over 85% of the children. Not bad at all. Also, six cats jumped out of the engine of our vehicle. That's less than 32% of our cats. Not bad, either.

As happens, I had a sibling missing a shoe. This time it was Rebecca. So, out of the vehicle we jumped. Some ran inside the house to look. Some ran outside in the yard to look. Some just ran around for the heck of it.

"It's here by the chicken coop!" I shouted, ever the hero.

The shoe was *beside* the chicken coop. It turns out my brother Sam was *in* the chicken coop. He was the missing 15%.

Sam was throwing eggs against the wall. Or trying to. His church clothes were restricting his arm's throwing motion. Most of his throws sent eggs towards the ceiling, where yolk and shells dripped down onto his hair and clothing. He was having a grand old time. Made me jealous. Until my dad yelled at him. Made me not jealous. Mom and Dad got him cleaned up mostly and, after chasing a few more cats out of the vehicle, off we went.

We were expecting to see new people this Sunday. You see, whenever something terrible happens, people seem to think they should go to church. Like God is an oil change center for your car. Come when needed, and then ignore God for months or years afterwards. I don't think God is like that. If anything, God is like a chicken coop. He feeds us. He puts us to work. He surrounds us with craziness. He is a place of comfort where you can throw eggs, smile, and somehow be at peace.

We walked into the church; the service had not yet started. To the front we went. The big family always sits at the front. I imagine there's a particular sign at the front of every church: *Reserved for the Big Family*. Maybe it's so that the big family will be a light for the rest of the congregation. Maybe it's to put the big family in sight of everyone, to make the children behave. Maybe it's just tradition, like a bride wearing white or a kid losing a shoe before church.

There were new faces that Sunday. At least faces that hadn't been there in a while. Like Christmas and Easter.

As I entered our pew, I looked over and saw a man with his two sons. The sons were around my age. The man was staring at us. I thought only babies stared unabashedly at others in public. The man started laughing as he stared. His curly hair made him look halfway between a clown and an adult doll. He leaned back and said something to a man behind him. I heard it.

"All those kids belong to them?"

I blushed as I sat down. Our church, a tired and plain structure, seemed old and dying. Best to make fun of the vibrant family with kids, right? It hurt.

The church looked comfortable that morning. The wood rafters breathed a familiarity; the stained windows gave illumination and a sense of being set apart. I looked around and noted the spot where the cleaning lady once dropped a hot iron on the carpet. I counted how many light bulbs were out on the chandeliers. Same as two weeks ago. I stared at the candle that once lit an altar boy's hair on fire. He was nodding off while holding it. It woke him all right. Set off the fire alarm, too. Good memories.

Everyone stood up, and the choir began singing. I reached for my watch, flipped it to the stopwatch setting, and started my weekly task. I time the music—don't tell my parents. Some weeks we're there for an extra thirty-two minutes because of all the singing! Oh, there are good people in the choir. I would just prefer to get home thirty-two minutes sooner, that's all.

As I was working my stopwatch, I looked at my brother Josh. He smiled and held up four fingers. I smiled back and nodded. My dad caught me glancing, and I snapped my face back to the front. Four meant how many chins the big man in the front of the choir had. Very rude, I am sorry to say. I know better. I've come to understand that a church isn't filled with saints. It's filled with sinners. Sometimes, the sinners even sin while at church. It's like going to workout at a gym but eating a dozen doughnuts there instead. I am one of those guilty of this—the sinning at church part.

The song ended. The Mass continued. At one point, I saw Sam chewing gum. His smile said it all. Not only was he having a forbidden treat, but I could tell he had procured the treat from the underside of the pew. Gross.

Soon enough, it was time for the priest to preach. Father Wally stood before us, a pleasant man in his forties with glasses, kind eyes, and messy hair. His full name is Father Wally Zsxyltchovskiwehveltskibetishly. I may have missed a consonant or two. Father Wally's not originally from Canada. Either he's Polish or British. I think it might be Polish because he mentioned perogies once or twice before. Father Wally seemed weighted down this particular Sunday. His kind demeanor appeared stressed. I took note and did something unexpected. I actually listened to the sermon.

"My beloved," he spoke with a trace of an accent, "these are times of great suffering for our town. I'm sorry to have to report a few things. Our mayor asked me to do so. We lost two men from our town in the explosion. All the same, I can't help but believe that this is a miracle. It could've been far worse. Several business owners had closed their shops to go on some errands. I think it was the hand of God.

"As I'm sure you heard, they struck a gas pipe while working with excavators. Half of our downtown is destroyed. It isn't easy to look at. It's difficult not to ask, 'Why, God? Why?' What will happen? I've been talking with some. It's hard enough to make a business successful in a small town. But to start over from scratch? They don't know if they can rebuild."

I was stunned. I didn't realize it was so severe. It made sense, though. It's hard enough to make a small business work in a town on a good day; how was someone supposed to rebuild first before trying the same path?

Father Wally continued. "They are devastated. We all are. Our town is in trouble. It's like when the apostles fished all night and returned without any catch. Oh Mamamia, what trouble they had! And then Our Lord had them launch into the deep. They caught fish! And, and, uh..."

Father Wally's voice drifted off. His eyes were downcast. He wasn't fooling anyone. It was all coming down on him, you could tell. This old town might not be able to handle this accident. The air was sucked from the room. Being eleven, it felt awkward. I looked at Sam. Even he had stopped chewing his gum. Suddenly, Fr. Wally's eyes perked up. He breathed in deeply. New life entered. A fire was lit.

"Fish... fish... I have it! My beloved. We need to go fishing! I mean it! Fishing will save the town. What I mean is God will use our fishing. If we all go fishing, I know one of us will catch a monster fish. We can sell that fish to raise money. And the news will be buzzing. Everyone will want to come here to fish. The town will *have* to survive! I heard about a town in the United States once having that happen. Saved everything! Yes, we all need to go fishing. Today! Come with me to the river. Let's hurry on with the Mass so we can get out of here!"

It wasn't the most logical plan I ever heard. The fact that we could race out of the church interested me. In fact, he cut off the choir when they started singing again. It messed up my timed-singing statistics, but in a good way.

Soon enough, we left the church and entered the warm morning air. My parents were chatting with other grown-ups. A few of my siblings were running around with their friends. I went to the vehicle and waited. Watching others play made me sad. I can't really describe it. Like I want to be happy, but not. Does that make sense? Yes, I can't really describe it at all.

I noticed a man leaving the church. I'd seen him before. He was a regular. Yet I didn't know who he was! He looked kind of creepy. Old, with a mustache and jacket. He wore a pair of work gloves. I don't get it. He walked right past everyone and down the street. It reminded me of something I would do. I shuddered. Was that going to be me someday? I made a vow right then and there. If nothing else, I vowed never to randomly wear work gloves in public.

On the way home, my mom asked, "So what are we going to do today?"

"Go fishing!" answered my dad.

We fished—just us and Father Wally. No one else came. He let us keep all the fish he caught. A good thing about having so many children is you rarely have to worry about legal fish limits. But no monster fish. Father Wally looked disappointed, so we invited him for a fish fry. Good food.

Good company. I'll take these sorts of disappointments any day of the week.

However, we still didn't help our town any.

Chapter Six

Marty

Saskariver has a local celebrity. How it came to be seemed ordinary enough. Just like any other place. Things escalated. Now, the rest of the world thinks we're weird. Sigh. I'm a misfit living in a town of misfits.

Two years ago, around March, this celebrity showed up. However, he was unknown at the time. His name was Marty. Marty was cold and hungry. He needed a meal or two and some love and attention. Is that so bad? So, Marty happens to be a moose? So what? Moose are people too, you know.

That March, Marty ran by the elementary school. It was during recess. A few hundred kids, wearing snowsuits, mitts, and toques, ran towards Marty as he crossed the field next to the playground. The teachers threw a fit. They were blowing whistles, calling 911, and threatening to contact parents if the students didn't back away. I guess Marty was putting on a show, and the students weren't leaving. Marty came racing towards the playground. Cheers erupted. Marty wanted to play.

Marty started chasing a grade one teacher named Mrs. Lumsden. Mrs. Lumdsen screeched like an infant girl, and

Marty took that as a sign to continue playing. Around the slide structure they went. Marty would turn and follow Mrs. Lumsden. She would duck the other way, only to be met by a long moose snout. Back and forth they danced. I'm told it was quite the sight, just as-is. However, Marty did something that put him into legendary status. He stopped chasing Mrs. Lumsden and, with a smirk on his face, leaned his big brown behind against the smooth red slide. Marty dropped the most enormous pile of poo pellets ever seen. Right on the slide. Turning his gaze towards the crowd, Marty opened his mouth and bellowed out what eye-witnesses call an earth-shattering guffaw. That is to say, Marty laughed. Like a giant blowing on a tuba with a kazoo caught inside the piping. A majestic moose laugh. With that, Marty trotted away.

Wouldn't you know it, the entire school was placed in a lockdown drill for the remainder of the day. Students had to remain in their classrooms until the conservation officers showed up. Two years later, the conservation officers still haven't caught Marty. As for the poo, it froze on the slide and remained there for another month. The slide became a monument to Marty. No one's used it since. What a legend.

Since then, Marty has made many appearances. So much so that people hardly even notice him anymore. Once, Marty crashed Jennie Book's 100th birthday party at the Pinegrove senior home. He went right through the front door and to the back garden area. The front door was closed at the time. He literally crashed the party.

There was a group picture happening. Family and guests surrounded Jennie—fifty people or more. Just as the camera shuttered, Marty came bursting in. He stole the piece of cake from Jennie's dish. Jennie shrieked, which surprised everyone since Jennie hadn't spoken in ten years. Marty laughed back. Jennie joined in the laughter—a touching scene. Marty and Jennie had an instant connection. He visited a few more times. Usually when cake was involved. When Jennie died a year later, there was another touching scene. Marty was found lying down at the cemetery, right on top of Jennie's grave. He honored her in life and death. I'll say it again: what a legend.

I'm sorry to say that sometimes people are jealous of celebrities. After the explosion, one poor, messed-up soul in Saskariver thought it would be a fun idea to plant parts of a moose near the debris-filled downtown. You know, to suggest that Marty was killed in the explosion. Not that funny. The police later confirmed that the moose parts were actually from nearby roadkill. Some doubted this claim. That is, until Marty showed up one day to prove that reports of his demise were greatly exaggerated.

🍁 🫎 🍁

When something devastating happens, having support from others feels good. I can't describe it. Compassion? Empathy? Like when my uncle died years back. A baseball coach pulled me aside and told me he was sorry for my loss. I swear I was choking back tears when he said that. It felt right. I was willing to run through a wall for that coach.

Saskariver, I think, needed some support like this. Like a hand on the shoulder and a few words of sympathy. Just an "I'm sorry for your loss" from the rest of the country. Well, the explosion did make national news. But that soon faded. I'm told this type of news is called *The News Cycle*. It's here today—then someone shouts, *Squirrel!*—and it's gone tomorrow. *The News Cycle* was now covering other vital events like the birth of a cute baby seal off the coast of Newfoundland or the eighth divorce in ten years of some movie star. Meanwhile, my place on Earth, Saskariver, was falling apart.

The Saskariver Chamber of Commerce, called the COC, took action. They do not represent the town or the mayor, just the local businesses, restaurants, and shops. I guess business was starting to hurt. We were going to lose a few places to shop. The meat shop. One of our main hardware stores. A clothing store. Other places, too, I imagine. So, the COC had a media day. They were going to have a fundraising barbecue with cake and coupons. Get the people out. Rally the troops. More than that, they invited television reporters from far away to cover the event. They wanted to keep Saskariver's struggles relevant not just for publicity's sake but for the sake of needing compassion.

It was roughly three weeks after the explosion. The barbecue was to occur at noon, midweek, at the somewhat-cleared-out main street near the explosion site. My mom said we could go. Even Dad would be there, having come from his work across the river. School kids were brought as well. It was a real event.

"Go say hi to some of your old friends," said my dad.

I slinked away and stayed near my younger siblings.

"Don't be rude," my older brother Josh added.

I guess that's why I'm seen as rude. It makes sense. I want to be there with others. But I just...can't. That's just being rude, right? I am a rude kid. Right? I'm shy, one-on-one. But put me in front of a television camera and...

Television cameras started scanning the crowd, and reporters were out in full force, doing random interviews with people who shouldn't be on television. Billy from the tire shop, who never found a curse word he didn't like, was giving a vibrant interview with one lady reporter. Her eyes bulged, and her cheeks reddened. Meanwhile, the cranky man with the green hat was giving an interview with another camera crew. He was complaining about his toilet problem, all on national television. Another reporter had managed to find Mustache to interview. Holding a cat, Mustache informed the world that he wondered if people in the town would be too lazy to rebuild, unlike him.

My older siblings joined their friends, while my younger ones stayed with me. At one point, a television camera scanned us. I did the first thing that came to mind: I opened my mouth to show the world my chewed-up hot-dog that was in my mouth. The camera turned away.

Wouldn't you know it, just as the atmosphere was really building, with music playing and laughter gathering, a special visitor arrived. At first, it was the mayor. She quieted down the crowd and started speaking while holding a piece of cake.

"My people of Saskariver. You are the beacons of bravery. The experts of explosion recovery. The kings and queens of conquering fears!"

Meaningless words.

Nutrine's eyes glistened, and she added, "Saskariver, you are a diamond in the rough! A real jewel of a town. I will always be thankful."

Now it was my turn to perk up. A diamond? Hmm.

A roar of cheers erupted. It wasn't for the mayor, however. While all the cameras rolled, Marty came trotting in. He came up to Mayor Nutrine and nipped the cake from her plate. The mayor's eyes bulged. Kids cheered. Marty turned and smiled for the cameras. What a celebrity!

The rest of the world wasn't ready for Marty. The news reporters and camera operators went berserk!

"Hello, Toronto! We're under attack. Ladies and gentlemen, Saskariver is a dangerous place!"

"We need to run, dear Canada! We are in grave danger! Just look at this menace!"

"Stay away, people! It's not safe here!"

The media personnel erupted in fear and chaos. They started running for their vehicles. Reporters were stepping over tables, chairs, and children, desperate to escape. Soon, there was the sound of shouts, tears, and screams. The party became a mini-riot. A hotdog cart spilled over. The bouncy castle got hit by a car backing up. *Poof!* it went, whooshes of air flooding from several tears in the fabric. Sirens went off. Car alarms screamed. Cats shrieked.

It wasn't a good day for Saskariver. In fact, I think it hurt a lot. Now, no one would want to help us out. We were too weird. Too misunderstood. Yet still, Marty stood there, eating his cake and smiling. What a legend.

Chapter Seven

"Shh!"

"Rick! They're coming from the left now, too. We need to split up. You cover the right side. I'll sweep over there. Give me half the grenade stash. And I need one more gun."

Bob was in trouble. The beginning of the end was not as he first expected. It was only a matter of time before the end of the end came. What could two men do against an army of five thousand? But Bob, like his brother Rick, never gave up without a fight. It is better to die with honor than live in fear.

"Uh, yeah! You do that. I go and get bad guys here," stammered Rick.

The two of them split. Their green soldier uniforms were worn and tattered. Their bodies were covered in dirt. Their spirits clung to the hope that every evil must pass for those who push through. Hunkered down in the woods, they fought. Shooting, whooping, army-crawling from one tree to the next. Always on the move. The enemy could never find them this way.

"Come on, Rick. There's two of us and maybe ten thousand of them now, but if we act like a big army, they'll get scared and flee!"

"Yeah. We be big fighter-guys. Pew! Pew!"

"Time to come to town!"

The fighting paused for a moment. This was not the voice of Rick and Bob. It was from the enemy side. Rick started shooting in its direction.

"Come on! It's time for your library story hour!"

Even soldiers need library story hour. More accurately, they need proper feeding, and to refuse library story hour is to refuse to be fed supper. These soldiers laid down their arms and surrendered.

❦ 🫎 ❦

No longer Rick and Bob, one late afternoon several weeks after the explosion, my brother Sam and I were to go to library story hour. Rebecca was to join us. I didn't want to go. The story hour wasn't for me, anyway; it was for the younger kids. However, in a large family you get volun-told to watch siblings. My parents say it's good for learning maturity and responsibility. I'm pretty sure fighting thousands of Nazis with just your little brother requires more maturity and responsibility.

The trip to the library was long. We got caught in a typical Saskariver parade. Ever been in a parade? I've been in dozens if not hundreds. Saskariver is a special place with at least three parades daily. They all have the same cause: Green Truck Guy. Green Truck Guy is the old man in the beaten-up green Ford pickup truck who drives the busy roads of Saskariver three times a day. He likes to watch people and things, to note the growth of the flowers and the development of the trees. He likes to watch kids play at the playground and dogs walk their owners across sidewalks and fields. The only problem with Green Truck Guy is he's slower than molasses rolling uphill in the wintertime.

We were caught in the parade. It was 3:30 p.m., and school was getting out. The parade was two blocks long. Everyone was looking to pass Green Truck Guy. He either didn't notice, didn't care, or secretly was a sadistic man who liked to see people cringe in discomfort.

We were far back in the parade. I swore I saw a Lumber Coop truck ahead. I had visions of Mustache driving along with the flow of traffic. He'd be muttering that it was fine being caught in the parade cause then all the other lazy workers would have to do something. I want to think Marty the Moose was part of this parade as well. I saw moose droppings along the way.

When we arrived at the library, I had to run in with my brother and sister to get to the story hour in time.

"Phew, we did it. We made it through," I announced dramatically as we entered the doors. "Green Truck Guy's out and about!"

"Shh!" greeted us from the main desk where librarian Miss Fancy Spudd sat. Miss Fancy Spudd was always here. I think she was born and raised at the library. Or maybe she was born here, and they built the library around her. She'd likely die here, though I don't think that's true. She'll never die. She'll always be here. Her red hair flamed a love for books. Her thick glasses proclaimed that her passion for books had taken a toll on her eyesight.

My siblings and I walked in a few steps. Sam tripped over his own feet, and I caught him quickly before he fell.

"Shh!"

I smiled an apology to Miss Fancy Spudd. She didn't look up from her work. So, I cleared my throat to say something. "Ahem."

"Shh!"

"Cough."

"SHH!"

A light step forward.

"SHHH! This is a LIBRARY!" she shouted at us in a whisper-yell, sweeping her right arm dramatically to the place we were in.

I looked at her. I looked at the rest of the library. We were the only ones there.

"Sorry," I whispered. "We're here for the library story hour."

"It's in *that room*!" She pointed ahead. *That room* was a room with a few more books, a large table, a picture of a young Queen Elizabeth II, and little else.

My siblings and I entered and sat in chairs overlooking the massive wooden table. We were entirely alone. Odd.

"Can I sneeze?" asked my little sister Rebecca. Her wide eyes looked concerned. Her dark hair rose in a static electric fear.

"Better not risk it," I said, almost inaudibly.

Sam let out some, er, gas. Loudly. It echoed across the table and towards the door. It had some odor to it as well. Just as Miss Fancy Spudd and two girls almost entered.

They didn't *fully* enter, for the pungency created a wall for them.

I would've been a bit embarrassed, but this time I was very embarrassed. The two girls with Miss Fancy Spudd were the Carnduff sisters. Evelyn was my age, while her youngest sister Rachel was six, like Rebecca. They both had shimmering orange hair, clear complexions, and vibrant blue eyes. I was in dirty sweatpants and a T-shirt that said something about throwing a policeman a doughnut to get away from him. Look, I'm just eleven. I don't care for girls. Especially Evelyn. I'd seen her before. I think she sometimes went to our church. Maybe sometimes she was at our youth group events. Maybe. I never noticed. Never. Nope. So, stop with your thoughts right now. You hear? I DON'T CARE! Which is why I immediately pinched my brother Sam for his gas expulsion. I mean, uh...

The girls sat at the other side of the table, far from us Storthoaks children.

"Oh, it's just us, girls," said Miss Fancy Spudd. "I want all of you to sit together over there."

Another Saskariver explosion occurred. This one came from the inside of my stomach. It churned. It rolled. It gurgled. Loudly. And towards our spot came Rachel Carnduff and her older sister. I felt my position in life at that moment. A homeschooled boy. Unknown. Seen as rude for being shy. Unwanted by the cool kids. Or was it I didn't want the cool kids? Oh, to be back fighting thousands of Nazis in the forest. Nazis didn't make weird faces if your stomach gurgled.

"Hi Rebecca!" said Rachel.

"Hi Rachel!" said Rebecca.

Evelyn and I didn't say anything to each other. This was awkward. What if I started talking? She might start *liking* me. Better keep silent.

Miss Fancy Spudd broke the silence. "Today's story is about a little ship that travels far away to a big sea. Does anyone know what it's like to go to a big sea?"

"Once, I went fishing on the river," said Sam. "Joey said we were pirates who ate birds and shot at girls!"

I noted the squirm Evelyn gave.

"Anyone else?" said Miss Fancy Spudd.

Crickets.

"What about you, Joey?" she added, ending my life simultaneously.

"Uh..." I stammered. Everyone was staring at me. My voice took on a nasal quality. You know what I'm talking about? If not, go to a computer programming and repair shop and speak to a worker there. That's the timbre my voice took on. "Well, I can't help but think about the HMS Wager. A former merchant ship the British Royal Navy purchased and registered as a sixth rate. That's the worst type of warship. It was with five other warships and two transports. They were trying to capture a Spanish galleon laden with gold. There were close to two thousand people on the ships. Sometimes, they would force people to join. Boys. Retired people. Grab people straight out of the tavern!"

I probably should've looked up to see the bulging eyes of Evelyn Carnduff. A voice inside my head was screaming for me to stop, that I knew not what I was doing. I continued.

"The expedition hit everything imaginable. Typhus. Chased by other ships. Scurvy. Back then, they still didn't know what caused scurvy. But it killed more seamen than all naval wars and shipwrecks combined. They even passed by lime trees in Brazil. They just didn't know. Too late for many of the sailors. Then it was onto the waters near Patagonia. The HMS Wager hit the legendary funnel of ocean currents. It was dangerous. Waves and everything. They lost contact with the other ships. Captain Davey Cheap had some men act as human sails, climbing a hundred feet up in gale-force winds. One slipped and plunged to his death. Eventually, the HMS Wager marooned on what is now Wager Island."

I continued. Of course, I continued. I discussed mutinies, Spanish responses, and the legality of belonging to a captain if you are marooned off the ship but using some of the ship's supplies to survive. Even the topic of salty local celery as a cure for scurvy was not spared in my explanation. In short, I was impressive. A devastating analysis. A sight to behold.

When it was all finished, I looked over at Evelyn. She was motionless, taking it all in. Her eyes were staring at me. There didn't seem to be much life in those eyes. Like a sad puppy who knows each new morning brings but another day tied up in the yard. Evelyn's cheeks were pale, cold even. Finally, she spoke.

"You're homeschooled, right?"

"What's it to you?" I answered, feeling defensive.

"That's, um, quite the story about going to sea," said Miss Fancy Spudd.

"I think Rachel and I need to leave," Evelyn interrupted. "It's late. Thank you."

With that, they walked out, just like that. My story didn't impress Evelyn after all. Let's be honest: it chased her away.

Miss Fancy Spudd looked at Rebecca, Sam, and me. She sighed. Apparently, she does have some emotion.

"This is *it* for story hour." Her voice was unusually shaky. She removed her glasses, something I'd never seen before, and rubbed her moist eyes. "I'm afraid fewer people have been showing up. It's to the point where I think we need to cancel it. I'm not sure what's going on. No one's out and about anymore."

Thus ended library story hour. I felt bad.

Moral of the story: I should obey when the librarian says, "Shh!"

Chapter Eight

School's Out

School was ending at real school. For us homeschoolers, it ended weeks ago. Reason #2,543 to homeschool. Except we had to do more garden weeding at home as the older siblings did little, if anything, while finishing their school year.

It had been a couple of months since the explosion. The consequences of the blast were starting to rear an ugly head. If the heart of your town ever blows up, I have some solid, expert advice: Don't take it lightly. Saskariver wasn't in for an easy recovery. Saskariver was trending towards no recovery at all.

My mom, younger siblings, and I drove into town to pick up my older brothers and sister on their last day of school. Avoiding an hour-long bus ride to drive a few miles might be nice for them. However, we got caught in a parade along the way. Green Truck Guy was out soaking in the sunshine. Summer was here, and so was he. Behind him drove a who's-who of important Saskariver residents. For starters, Mayor Nutrine was close behind in a red convertible, honking, shaking her fist, and shouting things at Green Truck Guy like, "I'm the MAYOR! I can have you run out of town, old man! Don't mess with me!" She could be obnoxious when she wanted, which was usually most of the time. Behind her drove a dump truck, a combine, a twelve-passenger van, and fourteen SUVs of teachers leaving work early. Walking at a calm pace behind the last SUV was Marty the Moose. Marty enjoyed all crowds, that's for sure. What a legend. Behind Marty was Mustache, driving the Lumber Coop forklift. Finally, there was our large blue vehicle.

Mustache seemed sad today. Like he was lost in despair. Forlorn, even. Maybe he was having cat troubles. I asked Mom if I could go update him about our cats. This might cheer him up. She agreed.

Jumping out of our vehicle, I walked up to Mustache as he drove along—yes, the Green Truck Guy drives as fast as someone walking. On a good day.

"Hi, Mustache!"

"Huh, oh, yeah. Hey there. Yeah." The familiar trumpet voice of his sounded off-key today, like it was warming up to play for a funeral.

"Tony Skaponi's having kittens again," I informed him. "Third time this year. Now we'll have no mice around our place. Maybe some kittens will sneak over to the Lumber Coop, hey?"

Mustache smiled. "That would be great. Yeah. Can't say I'll be there, though." He shook his head with regret. "No. Yeah."

"Not be there? You going on vacation?" Then I gasped. "You won't work across the street at the Ramona Lumber Store, right?" Ramona Lumber Store was the evil big-business competition to the Lumber Coop. They had money and power. But they didn't have heart or clean-shaven workers named Mustache.

"Not those devils, yeah," he chuckled. "They ain't doing so good either. At least that's good. No, I guess I might be going on a really long vacation. Yeah. Thought the blast would be good for business. People needing supplies and all. Yeah. And I'm used to being so busy anyway. Doing all the work and all. Might as well let the busy work continue. Yeah. But no one needs lumber. No one is rebuilding their stores. No one's doing anything. Oh yeah. Scared. The Lumber Coop is emptying out. Yeah. Ron Spitballer says he'll have to fire all of us. Not like he says to us every day, though. This time, he means it. Yeah. He almost cried as he threw a radio at me this morning and told me to get to work."

"You can't be fired! I'll tell my dad! We'll build more chicken coops. We'll keep you in business." I said this, not knowing the financial cost of what I was saying, nor what need we would have for so many chickens.

"Thanks, Joey. Can't do it, though. No. Yeah."

The parade was winding right down the main street now. Or what was left of the main street. And just like a potato to the head, it finally struck me. The town *did* seem to be taking its sweet time in rebuilding. I pondered for a moment and shook my head. This darn town wasn't rebuilding at all. It was stagnant. Deflated. Defeated. Like a funeral procession instead of a parade. I was in a funeral procession.

"See the hardware store there?" continued Mustache. "The one that has no roof?"

I noted it. As though it took me a minute of searching to pick out the large building with no roof.

"Where's the roof?" he asked.

"In a million pieces, I thought," I replied.

"Yeah. But how long does it take to put a new roof on? Oh yeah. We got lumber where I work. I heard Bill, who owns the shop, isn't fixing it. He's not putting a roof on it. Yeah. They're gonna tear it all down. He got paid too much for the land. That's what I heard—heard it on Coffee Row, right here in Saskariver. So, it's true. I'll bet I know who paid him. Someone in our parade. Yeah. I don't mean Marty, either. Nope. Yeah."

This was terrible. No Main Street hardware store? What next? Was the town going to remove our one traffic light? Absurd. I walked alongside the forklift, contemplating the future. The downtown seemed cleaned up enough from the explosion. The building remains had been plowed into a large pile and carted away. The dirt and debris was washed off. All that remained was yellow police tape and small craters where basements of stores once existed.

"Are they going to rebuild all these stores that got blown up?" I asked. "Is anyone?"

"Doubt it. Yeah. I doubt it." Mustache pulled over in his forklift. "It's like there's more money in not rebuilding. Yeah. Well, this is my stop. I guess I'm supposed to help the town take down our traffic light. A job's a job. All the other guys at the Lumber Coop are too lazy anyway. Yeah."

We arrived at the high school, and Johnny, Josh, and Ellie were excitedly buzzing. School was out for them. I was pumped, too. Now, our entire family could share in the weeding of the garden. Though I, like Mustache at the Lumber Coop, did all the work anyway. Don't tell them I said that.

"What a day!" shouted Josh, as though we all weren't within four feet of him, crammed inside the family vehicle. "Stealing. Accusations. Threats. Fights. And that's just the teachers! Or the ones that stayed the entire day!"

"What?" asked Mom. "That's it, I'm homeschooling all of you!"

"No, Mom, it's all good," said Ellie.

"Not for Mr. Keestick and Mr. Mullet," said Johnny.

"Aren't they your teachers?" said Mom. "They teach all the gym classes. I thought you liked them. What happened?"

"Oh, they're the greatest!" began Josh, sitting tall in his seat. "It's just... Well... It all started when the principals went away for the day. They said something about meetings. I think they went to the spa in the city. Like last time. They all had tans the next day. So, the principals were gone, and Mr. Mullet took us to the gym, but there was a note on the whiteboard. It said—let me try and spell it out—'Wear's all the dogebals Mulet? Mr. K. is loking for them. STop takin them!'

"Mr. Mullet got all mad. He started flexing his muscles and telling us he never took the dodgeballs. He left a note for Mr. Keestick. 'Learn to right. U took the dogdballs. Giv them bak! Or face the ~~consekqencs conseqeuenses~~ my rath!'"

"Later in the day," added Ellie, "Mr. Keestick bribed our class with cake to not talk to Mr. Mullet when he came to bring us to the gym. The cake was good. Even Marty showed up. But Mr. Mullet got mad. He thought we were ignoring him, which we were. Eventually, he flexed enough that one of the boys told him Mr. Keestick told us to be silent. Well, he marched us right outside. Mr. K. was teaching a gym class. They had about ten dodgeballs and…"

"I'm confused," said Mom. "Just tell me what happened."

"We all saw this part," said Josh. "Mr. Keestick and Mr. Mullet challenged each other to dodgeball—just them and their classes. There were only ten dodgeballs, so some students started running and grabbing textbooks and school supplies to throw. The battle was on! By this point, everyone in the school came out to watch. We were all cheering for our favorite gym teacher. Some of the teachers snuck away. It was awesome!"

"I stayed in the computer lab, actually," interrupted Johnny, ever the computer geek. "I was able to have three computers running simultaneously. It was great!"

We were a mile or so from home now. Josh finished the story.

"Soon, the fight was turning right into a schoolwide riot. So, Mr. Keestick and Mr. Mullet did something to stop it. Instead, they challenged each other to fight. One-vs-one. In front of everyone! It was wild. Mr. Mullet kept flexing. Mr. Keestick would punch hard. Mr. Mullet would say it didn't hurt, though he said that in a weird high voice, and then he'd punch back at Mr. Keestick. On and on it went. A punch here. A flex there. A few pushups in between a big kick. It was about to get to the big finale when..."

"What?" I shouted, desperate for the result. We were pulling into our yard now.

"The principals showed up in their car. They came running into the fight. Mr. Mullet muttered something about dodgeballs. I guess the principals said they'd lent most of the dodgeballs to the elementary school for the day."

"So are Mr. Mullet and Mr. Keestick in trouble?" asked Mom as the vehicle stopped.

"All the students told the principals they were just doing a self-defense demonstration," said Ellie. "It didn't work. Well, it did, but it didn't. We just found out that the school is going to lay off a bunch of teachers. Including Mr. Keestick and Mr. Mullet."

"What?" said Mom. "What for?"

"Something about fallen registration, or too many people moving, low enrollment, stuff like that," said Josh, the realization starting to sink in. "I'm going to miss them."

"This blasted town's falling apart," said my mom.

"And without a fight," I said, flexing my muscles unconsciously, unaware of the foreshadowing wisdom of my words.

Chapter Nine

The Boy of Summer

I t's me again. Live. Guess what? I'm still in the grave. And guess what again? I'm not dead. I think you figured that out by now. Jesus never came. My aches and pains have drifted away. Now I'm just cold. Also, I remembered to check my pulse. My ticker's still running great. My brain? Not so much. My courage? It's nowhere to be seen.

Is it wrong for an eleven-year-old to contemplate death? I can't help it. I'm stuck in a grave, after all. This world can't be all there is. That would be like traveling halfway around the globe in anticipation of something great and wonderful, only to arrive at a burned-out warehouse with a sign saying: *This is all there is.* But what will life be like after death? I used to think heaven would be like a giant waterpark with a wave pool, two dozen or more waterslides, and no lineups to ride them. Even better, you get your own bedroom with a waterslide that goes right out to the main pool. Poolside pizza is for lunch. The temperature is always perfect. The excitement never leaves. There are never eleven-year-old girls around to talk to.

Maybe that's what heaven will be like. Probably not. Ultimately, I think heaven would be a happy place without the constant threat of change to worry you. I hate change. But I think it is needed, at least on Earth. Change lets us know we live in this world of time—we are bound by time. It must be so. To live where change isn't always pressing down on you, crushing your mind and shoulders, is, I think, to be at peace. I want that peace.

Right now, I don't have that peace. As you can tell, things are bad for my town of Saskariver. They're quickly getting worse, too. I should get back to my story. Where was I? I know. Do you like baseball?

🍁 🫎 🍁

There was one final event needed to truly kick off the start of what promised to be a bizarre summer. The senior boys' baseball championship still required playing. Saskariver was desperate for some good news. Let the boys of summer provide it. As it turns out, *boy* is the best word to describe at least one ballplayer.

"Are you ready? Get off the computer, and let's go," said Josh. Josh is super competitive.

"Just another two minutes," said Johnny. Johnny makes a better programmer than pitcher.

"Everyone in the vehicle," announced Dad. "Ellie, make sure there are no cats along. Joey, make sure there is a Sam along."

To town we went. It was the first Saturday morning in July. My oldest brothers were about to play in the championship game for senior baseball. Their team name was the Saskariver Chickens. Other towns make fun of us for that, but what can you do when your team sponsor is the Lumber Coop? And besides, it beats what the team used to be when the Esso gas station sponsored them. The Bruins, with a large *B* on their uniform. Or, more specifically, the Esso Bs. Saskariver Chickens is a fine name.

The competition was from Saskariver's rival town, Bigfort. No, it's not true that everyone in Saskariver spits when they hear the name Bigfort. That's a terrible accusation. We aren't *that* low class. On the other hand, yes, it's true that everyone in Saskariver calls their town Bigfart. We aren't *that* classy, either—the Bigfort Millionaires. Millionaires is a suitable name. That mega international business sponsors them, the Ramona Lumber Store. This means they have the best equipment and uniforms that money can buy. But we have heart, determination, and a secret weapon to win.

Yes, I said *we*. I'm only eleven. The guys playing are much older and bigger. They'd crush a little person like me. I'd be annihilated. Destroyed. A few specks of debris. *We*?

"Hey Marc," said Saskariver's coach, Mr. Macklin, to my dad minutes before the game began. "We got a big problem."

I was busy playing catch with my little brother Sam while listening to Coach Macklin talk to Dad. Sam and I always brought our ball gloves to these games. We liked to catch foul balls and then return the ball to earn a quarter—one game, I made $10.25. Tax-free, I might add.

"What's that?" asked Dad, determined to help. No sacrifice was too big when the town of Bigfort needed to be destroyed.

"We're short a player!" said Coach Macklin. "I just found out. The Lashburns and Zenons are the latest families to move from town. This explosion's killing us. Well, we're officially down to eight players. We'll have to forfeit! Just like that!"

"Short a player? How about a short player? Take Joey," said my dad, determined to help, no sacrifice being too big. Not even the life of his son.

"Joey?" said Coach Macklin.

"Me?" said, well, me.

"Put him in," said Dad. "He can throw and hit better than at least two of your players anyway."

"I guess we have no choice," said Coach Macklin. "Joey, my wife can get you a spare uniform from the van. We're starting right away. You go play center field."

Within two minutes, I found myself standing at center field. I had a uniform that went down to my knees. I pounded my right fist into my glove. My hat was pulled low. Mainly to hide from the Bigfort parents and players who were jeering me, saying I had a lovely dress, and so forth. There is no mercy in a championship baseball game.

You're probably wondering why Coach Macklin put such a little boy in center field. That's where the action is! Why not right field? What my dad said is a fact. I wasn't even the worst player on the team. I was probably slightly better than the left fielder Jared, and miles better than the right fielder Windermere. With a name like that, how could he not be bad at baseball? I heard Windermere once brought his Transformers toy set to right field while the game was going on. When a ball was hit his way, he transformed one of his characters into a rocket ship before chasing after the ball, making engine noises as he flew to retrieve it.

Crack!

Wouldn't you know it? First inning, and a hit was coming my way! More like it went twenty feet over my way and slammed hard against the fence.

"Get the ball, Joey!" screamed a few hundred frantic Saskariver residents.

I ran! As fast as my five-foot-minus-one-inch frame could take me, almost tripping over my uniform-dress. I ran so quickly that my hat went flying. I went to the fence, picked up the ball, and stepped into the most enormous throw I ever made. As the ball left my hands, I imagined it sailing over the second baseman's head and one-hopping to the awaiting catcher. Instead, the ball two-hopped in front of the second baseman. Still, it was good enough to keep the hitter from getting more than two bases from his swing.

"Whoa! Willie Mays!" shouted a few of the old people at the ballpark. I think that was a compliment. My knowledge of baseball history doesn't go much older than the Toronto Blue Jays.

Suddenly, I felt like I could do this. There was nothing to be afraid of! I could do anything with anyone of any age!

"Joey, you're up next to bat!" said Coach Macklin at the bottom of the inning.

I felt like a dog wanting to hide from a thunderstorm. I couldn't show fear. Not with everyone watching. Definitely not with my dad watching. My tongue felt my top front teeth as I gripped the bat and walked up to the plate. I could feel the spot where a baseball had once chipped both front teeth. That was in my own baseball league once. With a pitcher my age hitting me in the chops. When I crumpled to the ground, my coach said I could sit out if I was hurt. I told him I was hurt. Then my dad told me I wasn't hurt, so I told my coach I wasn't hurt. I stayed in the game. It toughened me up.

But this? I was about to face a seventeen-year-old pitcher from Bigfort! He was over six feet tall. He had a long mullet and a thick brown beard. I think his mouth was full of chewing tobacco. He was practically a man. He burped loudly as I approached the plate. I was about to die.

That poor pitcher didn't know what was coming his way. It was time to unleash Saskariver's secret weapon: my height. Or lack thereof. Being over a foot shorter than most players gave one distinct advantage—a minuscule, impossible-to-hit strike zone!

"Whatever you do, don't swing!" said Coach Macklin from the sidelines. I knew what he was saying. I was to earn a four-pitch walk to first base. So, on the first pitch, I did what any eleven-year-old in my situation would do. I swung as hard as I could.

"Strike one!"

"Hey, no swinging!" said my dad. It being the championship game, he added, "Or you'll be walking home."

"Ball one!"

Three more pitches, and I was on base. An easy walk! I could get used to this.

Our next batter was Windermere. He struck out with just two pitches. Yes, two pitches. He swung even before the third pitch was delivered.

The game continued, the heat rose, and the tension escalated to a frenzy. I had two more balls hit my way. I fielded them flawlessly. And another time, a ball was hit out towards Windermere. I beat him to the ball and made the throw to the first baseman. Windermere just pulled up his glasses and sneezed. Like it was no big deal to lose out to someone half his size. He was making me look good.

However, Bigfort was not to be taken lightly. They could hit and pitch with the best of them. By the bottom of the final inning, it was Bigfort - 7, Saskariver - 6.

My brother Josh hit a single with the first at-bat. Jared and our pitcher Kyle both struck out. We were down to our final out. The season was about to be over. I was to bat next!

A wise man once said that baseball is ninety percent mental, and the other half is physical. Everyone knew the strategy involved here. The mental approach was simple. Bigfort could walk me easily. I wasn't the problem. The problem was that Windermere was batting behind me. He'd be the easy out they needed. All they had to do was walk me, strike out Windermere, and they'd win the championship.

That same wise man who spoke on the mental approach of baseball also once said that when you come to a fork in the road, you take it. Well, I was at that fork, and it was time for me to take it, come what may.

My dad pulled me aside and laid it out for me. "You need to hit the ball. Put the ball in play. It's our only hope!"

Dad looked over at Windermere. Windermere sneezed. The sneeze made the wooden bat in his hand tremble, which gave the pathetic boy a splinter. The splinter made him drop the bat on his toes. He started dancing around on one foot. With that, he tumbled over and hit our giant water cooler. It knocked over and splashed all over our Lumber Coop baseball gear.

"Make something happen!" repeated Dad, and he meant it.

With the crowd standing on their feet, I walked up to the plate. It was easy taking eighty-mile-an-hour pitches to earn a walk. I would stand far back in the batter's box and let the pitches come. But now I had to crouch close to the plate. I had to stare the pitcher down. I had to be a man. Or I had to die trying.

The pitcher knew this. He smirked an evil smirk as only someone from Bigfort could. The first pitch came hard and fast. Still, it was a good one to hit. Only slightly high in the strike zone. My courage failed.

"Ball one!"

"Achoo!" cried Windermere.

"Come on!" shouted my dad.

"Come on!" shouted a girl's voice from the crowd.

I tensed up. My grip on the bat was hard. I took a few practice swings to settle down. As I swung, I looked over at Coach Macklin. He looked at me, touched his hat twice, pulled his nose once, and did a chicken flap with his arms four times. It was part of the team's secret code. Seeing as I was a new recruit, I had no idea what it meant. Maybe he was inviting us out for wings after the game?

"Swing and miss!" shouted my dad.

Not understanding, I stepped to the plate and took my low stance. The ball came in like lightning. I swung with all my might.

Whoosh!

A clean miss! But as I swung, the catcher got distracted and dropped the ball. My brother Josh was already running to second base for the steal and made it easily.

"Good job!" said Dad.

"Good job!" shouted the same girl.

"I just stepped on my glasses!" cried Windermere.

Before I knew it, we were down to our last pitch. It was a full count. Three balls, two strikes. I looked over at my coach for another secret signal. His head was raised to heaven; his hands were folded in prayer.

I looked over at Windermere. He was crawling on all fours by the dugout, looking for a toy he'd dropped during his latest mishap.

By now, I was beginning to understand the pitcher's ways. A higher leg kick usually meant a faster pitch, often a little higher in the strike zone. I needed to observe and be ready to swing quickly, a little high, all the while making sure I didn't get killed.

The high leg kick, the pitch, the swing, the...

Crack!

I did it! I made contact! The ball hit my bat!

"Run, darn it!" shouted Dad and everyone in the crowd not from Bigfort.

The ball sailed right through the pitcher's legs, through second base, and rolled out towards center field. My brother Josh was already approaching third base when I started running. I knew my brother was going to try to run home and score. I could easily get to first base, possibly second, by the time they noticed me.

Josh rounded third and put on the jets for home. In came the throw. The catcher caught the ball ahead of Josh—a sure sign it was about to be game over! With what little hope remained, Josh put his head down and crashed into the catcher.

"Oof!" gasped the Bigfort catcher as the ball squirted loose. Josh touched home plate with his behind as he fell over. The game was tied!

By the time anyone noticed me, I was on my way to second base. I should've stayed at first base. I knew I was supposed to stay. But desperate times call for desperate measures. Windermere was going to get out next at bat anyway. There was nothing to lose. I raced hard. The catcher recovered, scooped up the loose ball, and threw it in my direction.

Still dazed from the impact with Josh, the catcher missed his throw. The ball scooted out into center field while I, in turn, scooted to third. I was expecting a throw to come my way, to take me out at third base. It never came. I slid face-first into third base, taking in a mouthful of dirt. Standing up, I realized that the centerfielder had misplayed the ball and was running back to get it.

There's no time like the present to become a hero. Imitating my brother Josh, I put on the jets for home plate. As I picked up speed, running like a hurricane, I saw the ball arrive in the catcher's mitt. A mere four steps away from the plate, I lowered my head and prepared for impact. Like brother, like brother.

"Oof!" gasped the runner. Yes, I bounced off the catcher and flew back three feet. I was out. The catcher raised his mitt in victory. As he did, the ball squirted from the glove in front of us. He was supposed to control the ball upon impact. I wasn't out just yet!

The catcher dove for the ball. In doing so, he blocked my path to the plate. Standing in my way, he lunged forward to tag me. I danced to the right. He slid to my right side, and I waltzed back and to the left. I was a chicken, bouncing around, avoiding being taken for the slaughter.

Again, the catcher lunged to my left. I slid right. In desperation, he jumped forward. All six feet two inches of him. And my five foot minus one inch frame took the low route. That is, I slid forward right under the legs of the catcher. Heaving my body forward, I stretched for all I was worth. My left foot felt contact from the catcher's mitt with the ball, hitting it. This occurred at the exact moment my right hand touched home plate.

"Safe!" yelled the umpire. Tie goes to the runner.

The rest was a blur. Teammates raced from the dugout, at least those who didn't first trip over a sleeping Windermere. I was hoisted onto the shoulders of Jared and Coach Macklin. The team paraded me around all four bases while the crowd of Saskariver fans cheered like there was no greater feat in the history of baseball. I looked up at the adoring mob of fans.

"Good job, Joey!" came the distinct voice of that girl. She had both arms in the air and jumped up and down like a kangaroo. Her smile was the size of Australia. It was Evelyn Carnduff.

I remember blushing when my brother Josh shouted, "Who's she, Joey? Huh?"

I distinctly remember having my heart ripped from my chest a few minutes later. It came during the trophy ceremony. To present the coveted Lumber Coop Cup was Ron Spitballer. He had a microphone and was standing at home plate to make the announcement.

"Congratulations to the Saskariver Chickens who beat the Bigf...f..." Ron paused a second to ensure he didn't say the wrong word... "the Big*fort* Millionaires. I guess you could say that the Lumber Coop beat the Ramona Lumber Store. Hey?"

Ron paused again, expecting some enormous ovation. A few awkward claps ensued. He continued.

"You crowd of punks aren't smart enough for my wit. Anyway, the player of the game award goes to the sawed-off little runt we've all been blown away by: Joey Storthoaks!"

People did clap at this. I came out and received a card for a free slushie at the gas station. Not the worst prize ever.

"And now I present the Lumber Coop Cup to Coach Macklin and his team of little chickens!"

The roar. The buzz. The feelings of victory. Moments to live for. What could possibly go wrong? I need to stop thinking this.

"Uh..." said Ron, growing reflective as the crowd's roar faded. "I guess you players have another treat in store." He cleared his throat. His dark, scary eyes looked sad. "You'll be happy to know that you can keep your Chicken uniforms and pants. That's right, they're yours! Uh..." A pin dropping a mile away could be heard. Everyone was listening. "Uh... I regret to say that the Lumber Coop will

not be able to sponsor the team next year if there is a team.
The Lumber Coop..." he swallowed.

What was he going to say? Why was he so emotional?

"The Lumber Coop won't be around much longer."

CHAPTER TEN

SASKARIVER EXHIBITION

S ummer was officially here. I pushed Ron Spitballer's shocking announcement out of my head and looked forward to the next thing: the town fair.

The day of the Saskariver Exhibition arrived, and I was more excited than a chicken roaming in a field of worms. My siblings and I could hardly handle our chores. Weeding became a chance to throw dirt at each other. Feeding chickens turned into chasing the dumb birds around the pen, acting like a Kentucky Fried Chucklehead. Standing with a nose to the corner was a chance to sing country songs in falsetto. Yes, we were hyper.

At lunchtime, we drove in for the parade. Not a Green Truck Guy parade but an actual parade. With floats, candy, horses, and did I mention candy? Unfortunately, though the sun was shining and the sky blue like mountain water, there were fewer people this year. Fewer businesses. Fewer floats. The usual buzz just wasn't there.

Or maybe I was projecting my own feelings about the parade. As we arrived, I was enlisted by a family friend to walk the parade route and pass out fruit stand coupons. Not even good coupons, mind you. Ten-percent-off-apples kind of coupons. They paid me $20 to do this. Why on earth did I agree? Besides the fact that my mom said I had to? In doing so, I missed watching the entire parade. More than that, at one turn, I walked by and noticed a group of boys led by Clay Englefeld. I groaned and put my head down, hoping these boys would ignore me.

You see, I am homeschooled. But I wasn't always homeschooled. I made the switch over a year ago. It's not that I didn't get along with people or had problems with bullies. I just, well, made the switch. It seemed right. However, I see now that in making the switch, there were past friends who didn't or couldn't understand why. I see further that some of them grew in resentment. Resentment must be Clay Englefeld's middle name. That, or just Creep.

"Is that Joey?" shouted Clay as I walked by. Two other boys smirked at me.

I didn't look up.

"Hey, Joey! How's life at home with your mommy?" said Clay.

I looked up at him, heroically keeping my mouth shut, and kept walking.

"Aren't you going to give me one of those coupons?" said Clay. "You can't ignore me. You remember me, right? Hand it over."

I approached Clay and held out a not-so-coveted ten-percent-off-apples coupon.

He snatched it, read it silently—moving his lips while he read as though basic literacy sent his brain into overdrive—and then shouted for all to hear, "This coupon sucks!"

Yes. Yes, it did. Don't shoot the messenger. Everyone knew it sucked. As did my job at that parade. There's no twenty-dollar bill worth that kind of trouble. In fact, I would rather pay twenty dollars not to be near Clay and those boys. Red in the face, I raced ahead in the parade to inflict more of these coupons on the people of Saskariver. It was good to get home after that debacle.

✦ 🫎 ✦

Dad arrived home early from work the next day and told us it was time to go. We rarely went to the exhibition for an entire day. It costs too much to take a large family there. Instead, we went around 3 p.m. when there were no gate entrance fees.

"Honey, you have our chairs to watch the chuckwagon races?" Dad barked while carrying Lyda, Sam, and an oversized bag of cheap nacho chips.

"Yes," Mom called back, carrying a cooler, jackets, hats, a diaper bag, and our lovable kitten, Little Mustache. "Ahh! Joey! Take this darn cat off of me so we can go!"

I grabbed Little Mustache while trying to finish an apple in my other hand. He started purring. I should've put him down near the chicken coop. Distracted, I tossed him to the ground, threw him my apple core—he is wild for apples—and helped gather the final supplies. We piled into our vehicle and headed to town, singing falsetto country songs the entire way—or at least until Dad told us the next person to sing like that would be left on the side of the highway.

At the exhibition, our parents let us split up. I went with Sam to tour the sights and sounds. The first step was to buy some ride tickets. The second step was to run to the bumper cars. The third step was to inflict punishment on others.

There wasn't a massive lineup, so before long Sam and I were strapped together into a bumper car, ready to cause destruction.

I looked around and saw Clay on a bumper car. It's amazing how you can not see a guy for so long, and then suddenly, he's everywhere. Amazing in a morbidly disgusting way.

I whispered to Sam, "Hang on! I'm going to destroy someone."

Sam pulled his glasses close to his eyes and smiled. He was ready.

The ride began. I jerked forward. Back. Forward. Eventually, I got the hang of things and started cruising around. I wasn't interested in making contact with anyone else. I drove around, picking up speed and avoiding all other drivers. After two laps around the course, I found my target. Clay was wedged next to another bumper car. I had a perfect side shot at him. One that would jerk him with violence and sweet pain. A side shot. A cheap shot. Zeroed in, I approached. Faster. My eyes lit up like a Christmas tree. My smile grew like a field of weeds. Faster! Faster!

Wham!

I nearly got jolted out of my seat—out of my soul. Sam slammed into me from the impact. We'd been hit before we could do the hitting. We were the ones annihilated! We were positively destroyed! The hammer was now the nail.

Who did this? What monstrous menace could inflict so much pain? Glancing over, I saw a little girl drive off, barely large enough to see over the steering wheel.

"Don't tell anyone," I mumbled to Sam, embarrassed at being taken down by a little girl.

Sam wrinkled his nose, suggesting I might need to bribe him to keep silent.

The ride stopped, and we jumped from the car to the ride's exit. Ducking away from Clay, I took Sam to the Ferris wheel next. The lineup was short; within minutes we rose, fell, and rose again, high above Saskariver. One second, we could look down on the roofs of houses and see people resembling little ants; the next, we were crashing down to ground level. Up, in time to see remnants of the main street. Down, in time for my stomach to lurch and moan. Up. Down. Would this ride ever end?

When I got off, I stumbled to a bench and sat down. My hands held my head. I was spinning all over. Or rather, the world was spinning, and I couldn't get off. I suffer from motion sickness. Even the mighty Ferris wheel can get me.

"Joey. I wanna go again!" said Sam.

"How about I win you a toy instead?" I pleaded.

The exhibition barkers were calling, and we answered. The row of games was loud and vibrant. It felt dirty and dishonest being there. Like I was in a place I shouldn't be. As with every community exhibition, there is a dark side where money changes hands, where secret merchandise is available, where winning and losing are controlled, where cats go missing.

We walked past the ring toss, duck hunt, and dart throw stands. I looked to the end of the row and saw Clay and his friends hanging out by a miniature fish pond, so I stopped in my tracks. Right beside a basketball throw. This could be harmless enough.

I paid five dollars for three shots. Three accurate shots would win Sam a useless little stuffed toy. I fired away. The first was a perfect swish. Same with the second shot. The third shot was fair and true, yet it caught a piece of the rim and bounced away. Ridiculous!

I paid another five dollars—same result. I hit the first two shots clean, but the third wouldn't sink.

Now I was mad. That was ten dollars of hard-earned money spent for nothing! There was only one thing to do: keep trying.

When it was all said and done, I had zero prizes and fifty fewer dollars. All that remained was my twenty-dollar bill earned from walking the parade route.

"Let's go find Mom and Dad," I said to Sam. I wasn't disappointed at having missed my shots. Even I could've told you that the setup was rigged, that something happened with the hoop on the final shot to stymie a win. I was disappointed with myself. I was a gambler. A filthy gambler with no self-control. For some reason, I thought of soldiers gambling at the foot of the cross to win Jesus's cloak. How could they be so horrible? It was easy to picture myself as one of them. I felt sorrow, but couldn't quite mutter that I was sorry.

Turning to go find the rest of my family, I came face to face with a smiling Clay Englefeld and his group of buddies I used to know. Clay had chocolate and red icing on his face, dirty-blond hair, and a black bunny hug (in Saskatchewan, we call hoodies *bunny hugs*). Clay was larger than me by quite a bit. What he made up for in size, he lacked a hundredfold in intelligence. I mean to say that Clay wasn't the sharpest knife in the drawer—not the brightest bulb in the fairgrounds.

"You suck," said Clay.

I tried walking to the left, right, and backward, but Clay stepped in my way each time. From a distance, one might think we were dancing together.

"I mean, your basketball shooting sucks," continued Clay. "What's the matter? You can't talk? Homeschooling means you need your mom to talk for you?" He laughed aggressively, sounding like a badger choking on a chicken bone.

"They do something with the baskets on the third shot," I told him.

"And it took you a hundred bucks to find out? Here, let me show you."

Clay walked over and paid his five bucks. His first shot was perfect. His second shot rattled its way in. And the third shot? It drained. I couldn't believe it! Clay, evidently, was part of the *in* crowd of the dirty games row at the exhibition.

"I gotta go," I said as Clay picked out a toy giraffe.

"Where?"

"I'm late."

"For what?"

"Something."

"What something?" Clay asked. This might take all day.

"The finals of the chuckwagon races."

"That's where I'm going. I'll walk you there." I was not too fond of the way Clay said that.

We walked through the gaming row, around the Ferris wheel, teacup ride, and giant slide. Sam stayed close to me. At first, it was quiet. Clay seemed to be thinking. I imagine it took a long time to achieve a bit of thinking. Finally, he spoke.

"Who're you betting on at the chuckwagon races?"

"Who's in?" I asked.

"Three teams left. Ramona Lumber, The Saskariver Bible Community, or something like that, and I think the Lumber Coop still has their entry. Why, I don't know. I'm taking Ramona. You're probably cheering for the Bible group."

He chuckled at this. To Clay, being associated with something wholesome like the Bible was grounds for being mocked.

"I'm cheering for the Lumber Coop," I said. They were my kind of guys.

"The Lumber Coop's going out of business soon. Everyone knows Ramona's got their number."

"My brother drove a forklift at the Lumber Coop!" piped in Sam as he walked alongside.

"Fifty bucks says Ramona wins!" shouted Clay.

"No."

"Chicken."

"No thanks, I'm not hungry."

"I am. I mean, no! What? I mean that you're a chicken. Come on. Fifty bucks. Let's go."

I looked out onto the track as we approached the grand-stand for the races. I spotted a sleek white-and-blue chuck-wagon, pulled by four perfect black horses, and a fancy *Ramona Lumber Store* written on the side of the cart.

The driver was from out of town. Probably a professional rider from far away. Past this, I saw an older white-and-red chuckwagon pulled by a mix of different-colored horses, and a smaller *Lumber Coop* logo hastily painted across the cart. More than this, I saw Mustache sitting in the driver's seat.

"Twenty bucks!" I shouted back, unable to contain my excitement.

"Deal!" said Clay. "There's a minute born every sucker, er, one minute ever born. Er..."

"There's a sucker born every minute," I clarified.

"You just got borned," said Clay.

CHAPTER ELEVEN

A RACE

The grandstand was three-quarters packed. I suppose that's as good as could be expected. The evening sun shone a pinkish orange on the lush trees hugging the exhibition ground. The sound of whooshing rides and terrified screams sent waves of jollity across this town. The sweet smell of horse manure and candy apples added to the atmosphere of nervous excitement. At least for one day, this town was alive and ready for a thrill. The chuckwagon finale was about to begin.

I, thankfully, parted with Clay and took Sam to find the rest of my family. They were seated in the front row on the left side. Just like church. Only this time, I planned on paying attention.

"Hungry?" my mom asked. While it seemed everyone at the grandstand had grilled burgers, perogies and sausages, fries, pretzels, and slushies, my mom had a cooler of homemade sandwiches, cucumbers, and dried fruit leather. Again, feeding a large family at an exhibition can be pricey.

"Yes," I said, "but my stomach's kind of rolling around in me. Maybe later."

I took a seat and waited. The Saskariver Bible Community chuckwagon was finishing up a practice jog. There were rainbows and smiley faces painted on the side of the chuckwagon and the words, *Run so as to win the race - 1 Cor.9.* Their horses looked temperamental and mischievous, like they needed to be baptized or something. But the rider, a young man with a red beard, was all smiles. "Bless and amen!" he called to the horses. They tugged and jerked him violently at these words. Maybe the horses needed a full-out exorcism.

Ramona's chuckwagon was getting a last jog in as well. I didn't recognize anyone with the horse outfit. They often sponsored championship teams from other parts of the province. Ramona was never lacking in money.

The Lumber Coop's horses were finishing their last touch of exercise. Mustache wore a dark-blue windbreaker and a black hockey helmet. I could hear him calling out.

"Yeah! Just here, little guys! Yeah. If we win, maybe we won't have to shut down. You'd better give'r all you got. Don't be lazy like the other workers. Yeah."

Mustache pulled into place, where Ron Spitballer and a few Lumber Coop boys waited to guide him towards the first barrel turn. I could faintly hear Ron giving a few words of encouragement to Mustache and the horses. Words like "runt" and "fired" reverberated into the evening sky. Ramona and the Saskariver Bible Community also got into position. At this point, there is no lingering tension. Getting horses in position is hard enough, much less having them stand and wait. In the blink of an eye, a horn went off, and so did the horses. The race was on.

The Saskariver Bible Community had the inside lane. Charging to the first barrel, the horses prepared for the turn. One horse hesitated slightly, knocking the team out of unison, and the chuckwagon skidded its way around, chewing up valuable microseconds. They came out of the barrels towards the main track in last place.

"Golly gee willikers!" said the red-bearded driver with a worried smile.

And who came out of that first turn in the lead? The Lumber Coop! Mustache had made his turn cleanly—as did the Ramona Lumber Store driver—fast enough to be ahead and in the inside lane. Things were looking good. My wallet was about to double in size. Assuming Clay would actually pay up.

The horses sped around the track. The sound of hooves and hollers cracked and rolled. Occasional shouts from the drivers could be heard.

"Hah! Ride, or I'll kill you! Argh. Hah Hah!" shouted the Ramona driver.

"Golly! God bless!" prayed the Saskariver Bible Community driver.

"Yeah. Oh yeah!" trumpeted Mustache.

The teams were on the main stretch, quickly approaching the final two turns. Mustache was still ahead by a mustache. The Ramona team could not catch up. Not at this pace. I looked down the long front row of the crowd and saw Clay at the other end. Our eyes met. He was terrified, his candy apple shaking tremors in his right hand. I smiled at him. This was it! Mustache drove a team of horses like he drove a forklift. Nothing could go wrong.

I need to stop thinking that.

"Meow!"

I looked down at my feet to see Little Mustache staring at me. Our little kitty had caught a ride to town once again.

"Not now! Shoo. Get out!" I hissed.

"Little Mustache!" cried my sister Ellie.

Little Mustache looked in Ellie's direction. At that moment, a candy apple sailed from the crowd and over the fence. It came to rest on the track near the finish line. I looked over at Clay, and his hands were empty. He smiled back at me.

Off went Little Mustache after the apple. The little kitty ran under the fence, dodged a dozen cowboys, and stopped smack in the middle of the track's inside lane. Little Mustache plopped down, grabbed the apple in his, or her, paws, and playfully gnawed at this newfound supper.

My stomach was churning to new heights. This was about to be deadly. The horses rounded the final turn and headed to the finish line. Mustache had the inside lane and the lead. The only thing stopping him was a small cat bearing his namesake.

"Mustache! Watch out for Little Mustache!" I shouted at the top of my lungs.

"Yeah. Oh no! Yeah," said Mustache.

"What the $%#!" said the Ramona driver.

"Oh, fiddlesticks!" cursed the Saskariver Bible Community driver.

The horses flew towards the finish line, and still, that darn cat lounged on the track, twitching an ear and, I imagine, purring. I envisioned the splattered blood of Little Mustache bathing us in the front row. I contemplated what life would be like without that cat. I thought of the millions of mice moving into our yard now. I meditated on how angry my parents would be that I had not put the cat by the chicken coop like I was supposed to. I might need to run away from home after this.

"Whoa! Yeah. Whoa!"

Mustache was pulling back on the reins. He was pulling defeat from the jaws of victory. All to save our little cat.

"Yeah! Whoa!"

His chuckwagon skidded. The horses slowed, but not enough. Soon, the tail end of the cart swerved into the other lanes. The Ramona driver took his horses ahead, crossing the finish line just as Mustache veered behind into his lane, also missing Little Mustache by a mustache.

The race was lost. And still, Mustache fought for control. He swerved this way and that like an out-of-control snake. The chuckwagon started sliding off its right wheels. Only the left wheels touched the ground. Mustache flew his body onto the right side to balance the weight. The cart settled down before fishtailing once again. It bumped up, crashed down hard, skidding a few more yards, and stopped in a cloud of dust.

"Ramona Lumber Store wins!" shouted the grandstand announcer.

The crowd cheered. I groaned.

Mustache held his head in his hands and sobbed. "Oh Little Mustache! You shouldn't have done that. Yeah."

Having finished the apple, Little Mustache came over to Mustache and nudged his, or her, gentle white whiskers in Mustache's face. Mustache hugged the cat, and all was forgiven.

Clay came running over to where I was sitting. "Pay up!" he sneered.

I threw my last twenty-dollar bill, the one so hard-earned, at Clay and looked away. How could this day get any worse?

I know I keep saying this, but I really need to stop thinking that.

"Ladies and gentlemen!" came the cackle of Mayor Nutrine. She wore a large white-and-blue pantsuit outfit as if she went to the Ramona Lumber Store for her clothing. All she needed was a Ramona hat, and she'd be a regular employee there.

"What a tremendous race this was! I'm pleased to present the Ramona Lumber Store chuckwagon team with the twenty-thousand-dollar prize!"

A sob was heard from the Lumber Coop chuckwagon. Twenty thousand dollars is a tough loss.

"Saskariver," continued the mayor, taking the opportunity to make a political, self-serving speech, "it's been a difficult year. Many of you are concerned that businesses are shutting down and friends and family are leaving. But I know things are about to change. This town is a diamond in the rough. I have a plan that will save the day. And with tremendous support from places like the Ramona Lumber Store, we will come out even better than before!"

I think the crowd was supposed to cheer. No one felt like it. It got really quiet.

A horse neighed.

A member of the Saskariver Bible Community uttered, "Golly, Miss Molly."

A cute kitty purred from down on the track.

And another sob echoed, "We're done. Yeah. Sniff. Oh no! Yeah."

"Sorry," I whispered from my seat. It was my fault the Lumber Coop lost. It was all my fault. And for the second time that day, I felt deep shame.

Chapter Twelve

The Pool

Besides the pool, we didn't spend much time in town that summer. It was too depressing to be there. Imagine living in a beautiful home with a burned-out kitchen and living room. The rest of the place is fine, but the heart is barren. That's what Saskariver was like.

Consequently, I hadn't seen the Lumber Coop in a long while. But I heard they were starting to sell off their stock. That the end was approaching fast, not just for the Lumber Coop, I might add. Saskariver had already lost two gas stations, a clothing store, a shoe store, two farm supply stores, and several other places, including the Chinese restaurant. Boy, did people freak out when they lost access to artificially-flavored chicken balls and dry fortune cookies. And still, I heard the mayor was excited about the future. Almost bubbling in anticipation. Always the diamond-in-the-rough references. What did she know that we didn't? Politicians are so inhuman. So creepy. It's a wonder adults keep voting them into power. If I ran the government, I'd ban all politicians.

Summer gets away from you if you aren't careful. Days start repeating themselves in a like manner—a mindless, glorious repetition. Wake up. Chores. Weed the garden. Lunch. Go to town for a swim. Supper. Some family time. Back to bed. To some, this can seem tedious. To an eleven-year-old boy, there are always new adventures to live, new villains to conquer, and new troubles to create.

A week after the fair, my mom took Lyda on some errands and dropped the rest of us off for a swim. We would play games like making diving catches while jumping off the diving board or trying to understand each other's words underwater. Sometimes we knew people there, and my siblings would play with them. In this case, I might swim alone or with my brother Sam. I felt more comfortable away from others. I know, I know. This can be seen as rude. I swear I don't intend it to be. It's peaceful, just meandering about in the water, pretending to be a walrus or shark. Or a sailor from the HMS Wager struggling to stay above the crashing waves.

On this day, Sam was floating on two pool noodles while I pulled him along. We pretended there was a storm and he had to get his ship safely to port.

"Hang on, matey! The storm's a'brewin mightily!" I shouted.

"The storm is...BIG!" said Sam.

"You may have to make a landing on this lonely island!" I called back.

"Make landing from BIG storm!" said Sam.

"Bring the HES Wagner close to shore and unload what you can!" said a voice from behind.

I turned around to face Evelyn Carnduff. I couldn't tell you how long she'd been watching our nautical shenanigans. My heart skipped. I didn't love talking with others.

I *really* didn't love talking with a girl. And I *really, really* didn't love talking with a girl while older siblings might be watching.

I did the only thing I could do. I tried to pass her off.

"It's the HMS Wager," I said, hoping she'd turn and leave. Quietly, I continued my story. "The island's far, and we're tipping. We might have to abandon the ship and swim. Look at those sharks!"

"I'm a shark!" said Evelyn, making a shark fin with her hands. Sam started gigging and splashing as she tried to get him. And just like that, I knew she wouldn't leave anytime soon.

We abandoned the ship, evaded the sharks, got to the island, and built a shelter. We chop-chop-timbered trees—as every young swimmer loves—and caught and ate sharks to survive. Soon, we were rescued and brought back home to England. Sam loved it. I think it was fun, too. Though I don't think I'm supposed to admit that.

"You have a big imagination," said Evelyn once our play story ended.

"Um, I guess," I muttered. Talking about something real made it feel awkward.

"So..." she said.

"So..." I said.

"So..." she said.

"See ya," I said, turning to swim away.

"Hey! I was going to ask you something," she said.

"What?"

"Hey, it's Joey! He's allowed out of the house today! That's enough homeschooling for the day."

Evelyn and I turned to see Clay Englefeld swimming towards us. Amazingly, he had chocolate all over his face.

"It's summertime," I said. Now, I was really the center of attention. In truth, I wanted to be locked up in my home right then.

"What's wrong with school at home?" asked Evelyn.

"What's wrong with being around real people like us? Like normal people!" Clay shot back. I think some bubbles came up from the backside of his swimming trunks while he spoke. "Joey, did your mommy teach you how to count yet? Can you even count how many brothers and sisters you have?"

I think I snapped. Deep down, I believe I am not a punching bag for others. I am not a little stuffed toy to be squeezed and made fun of. Clay was awakening something that was already there, waiting to explode.

"Yes, she did teach me. Let me show you. I'll start by counting the rolls on your gut. One. Two. Three. Four..."

Evelyn burst out laughing. I'm glad she did, because I'm sure it distracted Clay enough so he didn't hit me.

"You think you're better than everyone!" shouted Clay. "Well, you don't belong! You can go back to your big dumb family!" With that, Clay splashed me with water. It was supposed to be hurtful. But we were already in a swimming pool, wet and accustomed to water in our faces.

Clay swam away from us towards the deep end. I think his bullying had more of an effect on him than on me. I think it was because he couldn't control me, and that bothered him.

"What a jerk," said Evelyn. "You know, we're not all like that at school."

"Whatever," I said. My mom always hates it when I say that. But...whatever.

"Whatever?" said Evelyn. "How about *whatever* you were talking about at the library that day? Remember the H-something-something Wager? You were going on and on. Like a weird homeschooler."

"Thanks," I muttered.

"Then I saw you at the baseball game, whipping those bigger boys. And at the exhibition, talking with that Lumber Coop driver after the race. Like you know how to be cool with the best of them. Who are you, Joey Storthoaks?"

I let the words hover over the water for a few moments. Who is Joey Storthoaks? How could I say? I'm only Joey Storthoaks.

"Did you start talking all weird at the library on purpose to kind of..."—she blushed—"put me off?"

A no-doubter. Half-court swish. Hammer on the nail. Direct hit. Pow. I turned red.

"Maybe."

"You're a jerk."

"If you don't like it, then..."

"Joey. Maybe you're more normal than you think."

I looked around and saw the pool. A little kid threw a dry towel bag in the water while his mom freaked out. Another kid was picking his nose and eating the fruit of his labor. I looked out into the town. Green Truck Guy was leading another parade while Marty trotted behind. An old lady walked by with ski poles and a heavy sweater, even though it was summer. And I thought of the world. With all its crime, pain, and hunger. Where people sell their souls for a touch of money or five minutes of fame. Normal? Who wants to be normal? Whatever normal is supposed to be.

At that moment, I noticed Clay storming off. Judging by the angry look of the lifeguard, he was being kicked out of the pool. He stomped off to the change room. Evelyn and I both stared as he left the area. After a few seconds, I looked at Evelyn. Normal? We'll see.

"I gotta go."

"See! You're doing it again," she said.

"Yeah," I said, not at all thinking about what she said. I was in my own mind once again. A familiar, comforting, and bizarre place to be.

I hopped out of the pool and carefully went to the change rooms. I could hear yelling and swearing coming from the main change area. I paused and waited. After a minute, the curses became sobs. Clay was crying in self-pity. I peered my head around the corner.

Clay was getting changed all right. He was sitting on a bench facing the opposite wall; his towel and clothes bag were tossed in a pile behind him. He was trying to put a sock on. Other than the sock, all he had on was his underwear. I would tell you they were tighty-whities, but I don't want that image of Clay to be in your head.

Normal? I swooped in. His sobs and mutters drowned out my stealth movements. I scooped up his towel and clothes bag, turned, and ran back to the pool. Stepping out into the sun with Clay's items, I rushed over to the far fence, past the beach chairs, and chucked his items over the fence, out of sight.

"What was that?" said Evelyn as I jumped back into the pool.

"Nothing."

"You're the worst liar I've ever seen."

"There are worse liars than me!" I lied.

Clay came running out of the change room with nothing on but his undies and a scowl. People started laughing and pointing at him. When he realized this, he ran back to the change room. Normal bullies are so strange.

"Aren't you worried he's going to get you back someday?" asked Evelyn when things calmed down.

"He can't hurt me here," I said. "I know how to count. I've got two more older brothers than Clay has. He wouldn't stand a chance."

Evelyn shook her head and swam away. There was a crease of a smile on her face as she left.

At first, I felt guilt, but then I realized something. Standing up for yourself should be normal. A good kind of normal. I felt proud.

This lasted all of two minutes. Then I felt guilt once again. Normal or not, I took it too far. I know I did. Clay is just a boy, like me. What's that saying from the Good Book? *Do unto others as you'd have them do unto you.*

Yes. I took it too far.

Our summer routine of afternoon swimming lasted just one more week. A mayor's bulletin was posted on the swimming pool's main door.

Attention users of the Saskariver Eileen Womanly Memorial Northeast RecPlex Community Aquatic Recreation Facility at West Central Park:

We regret to announce that due to recent staffing issues, as well as plummeting attendance at the Saskariver Eileen Womanly Memorial Northeast Recplex Community Aquatic Recreation Facility at West Central Park (from henceforth to be referred to as the pool), we will be shutting down for the remainder of the summer, effective immediately.

It is uncertain if the pool will reopen next year or at any future date. There is too much financial strain.

Mayor Karen Nutrine offers her caring, courageous, and most sought-after support to all staff and community members affected by this decision. She reiterates that the pool has been a shining gem in Saskariver, "a true diamond."

Sincerely,
Bob Yorkton
Town Administrator

I thought of how I stood up for myself against Clay. It felt...invigorating. Maybe I needed to stand up for Saskariver, too. If not me, then who? Was anyone willing to fight for this town?

CHAPTER THIRTEEN

GOODBYES

"My beloved, we need a miracle. I guess we came to the right place. Haha. I mean. Uh. My beloved, we're in trouble. Grave trouble."

It was 11:23 on a cloudy Sunday morning. The choir had sung fourteen minutes and thirty-two seconds thus far. Our fearless pastor, Father Wally, was preaching another sermon. His flock was shrinking—his hope was nearly gone. He looked drained. Like not enough peanut butter spread over too many pancakes. If one is inclined to put peanut butter on pancakes. I am. With maple syrup on top. A glass of milk, too... As you can see, I get distracted easily at church.

"My beloved, you know our numbers have never been very high. We always got by, though. Since the explosion, we've been going downhill fast. We've done some fundraising. A bake sale. The fish fry. The garage sale. The bingo night. The second and third fish fries. It's only slowed the bleeding. Now we're reaching our last few drops of life."

I was all attention once again. What he was saying was foreign to me. How could a church just shut down? That sounds impossible. Like putting too much ketchup on French fries. You can always sop up more ketchup. It's just so sweet and savory and...

"My beloved"—Fr. Wally paused, removed his glasses, and wiped his eyes before placing the glasses on his thin nose—"our mayor has offered us a healthy payment for our church. If needed. Our finance council tells me it's a very healthy payment, strong enough to keep our flock together. At least meet elsewhere. Maybe gather weekly at a barn or even rent a hall on Sunday mornings. We, the people of God, don't need to be scattered. But it might look different."

"Impossible!" shouted the local beekeeper, Mr. Garzy. "We can sell more honey! Have a honey festival. I can dress up in a bee suit and pretend to fly to flowers and..."

"We'll have a concert to raise money!" interrupted Veerna, the choir director.

"Or a beauty contest!" added old Mrs. Mabel.

My mom pinched me hard as a laugh escaped from my mouth. I should stick to daydreams about food.

"We can raffle off a quilt," said old Mrs. Pearl. "I've got enough dirt on people in town that they'll *have* to buy a ticket, or I'll squeal to everyone!"

Now, it was everyone else's turn to laugh. It was funny. It was also very accurate.

"We can have more faith," mumbled the creepy guy with gloves. The church got quiet. Awkwardly so. This was no time for faith! It was time for nickel-and-dime ideas to save the church. And who was this guy anyway?

"My beloved, we've tried these types of ideas. You know we have. We're running out of time. In fact," he continued, pulling out a piece of paper and reading from it, "it's come to this. Here is a message I'm supposed to read: Mayor Nutrine invites the entire town of Saskariver for a special announcement this Tuesday at eight p.m. There'll be cake and fireworks to follow. It'll, ahem, be on the main street. My beloved... I think it means we've reached the end."

His voice trailed off. He was trying to sound upbeat. There was nothing left. All his fishing for a monster catch had proven fruitless, though it *did* provide enough fish to feed five thousand.

"My beloved, let us kneel and pray."

I'm sorry to say my mind drifted off again. When I zoned back in, the choir was halfway through another hymn. I forgot to track the time, so I scrunched up my paper, disgusted, and zoned out some more.

I thought of other things besides food. I thought of the loss of the swimming pool. Teachers laid off. People leaving like there was a plague. The Lumber Coop coming to an end. The shoe store. The Chinese restaurant. All of it. And now this church? Where will souls be saved? At home in front of the television?

And why did the mayor want us to meet on Tuesday evening? At that big, gaping hole called our main street, no less? We were supposed to gather there? With cake and fireworks? It felt like being at one's own funeral—a cool thought at first. People crowding around your body and saying nice things like, "What a great guy! Crafty and wise too. Yep, he'll be missed." A corpse could start smiling with such praise. But then a final goodbye is given, the final coffin nail driven, and you are lowered. Until the end of the world. Dying a premature death is not so cool after all.

No. I believe death is sad. I also believe the death of a town is worse. I don't think a town will rise from the grave the way a human person will. You only get one shot at saving a town.

The choir was now singing the final hymn—one about peace flowing like a river. Just to be defiant, I flipped to a different page in the hymnal and started singing the first words I saw on the page. They were much different. "Onward Christian soldiers," I sang, "marching as to war." My mom gave me *that* look.

So what if I felt like fighting back—homeschooled misfit, not-normal boy that I am? Is it not better to go down swinging? To not give up without a fight? What could possibly go wrong?

I *really* need to stop saying things like that.

"Can I take my bike to town?" I asked my mom that Tuesday morning. It was a risk. I was supposed to be out weeding the garden.

"Why?" she asked.

I should've been prepared for this obvious question. I wasn't. Instead, I panicked. I told her the truth. "I want to say goodbye to the town."

She looked up from scrubbing carrots at the sink. I could tell this answer surprised her. A few new wrinkles appeared on her face. Her hair, for a moment, looked more gray than brown. Looking back at her work, scrubbing with anger or an upset heart at what was happening, she nodded.

I bolted before she could change her mind. My dark-green bike with the cushion-gel seat—my poor delicate behind hurts when riding a bike—flew out the gravel driveway towards the highway. The wind is stronger on the highway. Out in the open of the vast prairies, it blows hard. My face grimaced with effort as the wind plowed into my face. My legs burned with exertion. Every thrust forward was like pushing the world down under me. Why was I doing this?

The *BOB'S CUSTOM GLASS* sign, without the *GL*, greeted me as I pedaled into town. Bob's glass was not in demand. His business was closed more often than it was open lately. People could go to Bigfort for glass. Bob was expendable.

I biked down the small hill, around the empty park, and past the post office. No farmers were hanging outside the doors. Just a lonely car pulled into the angled parking spot. An old man sat in the driver's seat. He did not get out. I imagine he was waiting for someone else to come. Someone to talk with about crops and taxes and which football team needed a new quarterback. He would have to wait a long time.

Onward, I biked. Past the empty lot where the hardware store once existed months prior. I thought of walking into the store on that unforgettable day a year ago. My pocket was full of two years' worth of savings. Two years! I came out with just two dollars to my name and this dark-green bike. I rode it home that day with the wind at my back. I remember raising my fist in triumph as I pulled into the yard. Sam was there to greet me. He raised his hand in triumph as well. Maybe he will inherit this bike when he's older. He won't be able to buy his own like I did. Not in Saskariver.

My bike was carrying me further into the emptiness. Past the shoe store and clothing shop. They used to sell sporting goods when winter came. I got my first brand-new pair of skates there. To not wear hand-me-down skates was to be like everyone else, to be normal, or so I thought. You might think I'm being dramatic or sentimental, but those new skates made me feel special. They were gray and black with neat yellow edges. I pulled them on, laced them up, and skated 100 miles an hour. But boy, did they give me blisters! Used skates have their perks, too.

Green Truck Guy drove past me, coming from the other direction. There was no parade behind him. Just him. He looked out with a dazed expression. Like the purpose of his life was missing. To force people to slow down. To stop and smell the roses. To chuckle at ourselves and stop taking everything so seriously.

Past the Chinese restaurant. A large *Four Sail* sign rested on the front window. Four sails to bear that restaurant away to a new town. To take the memories and melt them away, like fried shrimp dissipating in your hungry stomach. I thought of when my cousins and I made a drink with all the loose sugar, salt, pepper, hot sauce, and juice we could get. It tasted like death in a cup. I smile, thinking about my cousin, unable to talk for the next hour after tasting it. Can you even have a small town in Saskatchewan without a Chinese restaurant?

The empty section of our main street was next. I'm already forgetting how many businesses used to be here. They say a traumatic experience will take your memory away. To lose my memory of downtown Saskariver is to lose a piece of myself. It must've been a dream. All a dream. And it's fading now. Fading away.

The traffic lights were missing. Our only traffic lights. Our bragging rights over all the surrounding smaller towns and villages that did not have traffic lights. Four stop signs were hastily posted on each side of the intersection. It should've been a disaster. No one in a small town knows how a four-way stop works. On a typical day, you could be caught there for hours. What did it matter? The main street was nearly abandoned.

In disgust, I looked back to where the explosion had occurred. This filthy, wasteful piece of destruction. This once-beating heart ripped out with violence, leaving the body to die in agony. I looked and, for the first time, noticed something peculiar. Two large red pipes were sticking out of the ground. Some strange equipment rested next to the pipes. Like they'd been drilled down for some exploration. To find something.

I needed to get away from our main street. Yes, the heart of the town was missing. I didn't want to be part of a heartless place. So, I took a turn and traveled past the corner gas station. It was one of the few gas stations still running. Danny, the award-winning gas station attendant, was cleaning a windshield. He probably was the reason why it was still in business. I wanted to stop in and buy a chocolate bar, but money was still an issue for me following the exhibition. Instead, I waved at Danny and pedaled by. Danny waved back. He looked lost in thought. I couldn't help but think he didn't need this town anymore. That his skills would be better served elsewhere. That we had nothing to offer. We didn't deserve an award-winning gas station attendant. Yet he was still here. At least for now. Why?

Past the pool. Dry. Drained of water. Empty of all life. Once the center of our summer fun. I thought of the first time I floated by myself. I thought of the time I first swam a length. I thought of the time I pulled out a boy struggling to swim. Did I save his life that day? I thought of Evelyn asking curious questions about my homeschooling. I thought of stealing Clay's clothes and his screams and cries as he ran out into the open in his underwear. Heard across this empty town. To be buried with it.

Biking past the pool, I did the parade circuit. Even bad memories were something to be treasured. This one house had a boy stick his tongue out at me when all I could offer him was a ten percent apple discount instead of a lollipop. And this other street was where old Mrs. B. got caught in the parade and rode for three blocks. People waved to her. She waved back. It was okay. We can laugh and understand and not judge what needs no forgiveness. A simple mistake. A cause for a smirk, a story, and an acceptance that without such occurrences, we would cease to be who we are.

Past where Clay encountered me. Right behind the poplar tree. Like he was hiding and waiting. Right there. Looking mischievous and powerful, just like he was at this very moment.

Shoot.

"Joey!" he shouted to me as I biked past. "You suck!"

I should've raced past. Straight to the police station and begged for a whole escort home. But I didn't. It was better to get it over with if he needed to fight me. That, or I had another reason to confront him. Doing so now might take his tighty-whities image out of my brain forever. Lord knows I suffered enough from it.

"That's a big sentence for you, Clay," I said, adding against my better judgment, "I see you're wearing clothes this morning."

For a moment, fire lit in his eyes. I thought my end was nigh.

Fear brought wisdom, or at least a touch of honest-to-goodness empathy. I quickly muttered, "Sorry for what I did at the pool." As soon as the words left my mouth, I felt better inside.

Clay took several moments to consider my apology. Then, in the blink of an eye, he calmed right down and said, "I probably should smack you. But I don't have time for that. We're moving."

"Where? Big*fart*?"

"No!" he shouted. "I mean, I don't know. Maybe."

There was a look of terror in his eyes. I didn't reply. I don't think I needed to. My own look said it all—one of shock, regret, and sadness.

"It's alright," he said.

"Sure," I said.

"I should go."

"See you around," I said. My voice nearly cracked.

I decided to do something heroic. I smiled. I couldn't believe it until it ended, but he smiled back. It was as close as two eleven-year-old boys can get to having a meaningful conversation. It was normal. In a good way. Suddenly, I didn't feel so different or unusual.

I biked on. Past the church. Where I was baptized. Where the large family should be the greatest sign of hope. Where every Sunday was an adventure. Where every stranger, misfit, and friend has, or *had*, a home. Past the cemetery. Where I once sat in the grave. Where I, as I tell this story, currently sit. Where I one day will lay down and never come out until a new heaven and a new earth break forth in clouds and trumpets blast. With no more tears shed. Only peace and security from change. Where no one is a misfit. Or maybe we all are misfits in a place too glorious. Freely given and undeserved. That is a vision of heaven far exceeding a thousand waterslides.

And finally, I biked to the Lumber Coop. Past the *Going out of Business* sign and right into the lumberyard. I cleared my throat lest I crack with emotion.

"Yeah, here's trouble," called a familiar voice.

Mustache and nine other workers were hanging out on a lumber pile. Hot Rob. Snoozy. Honkin. Hard Worker. All of them with a personality bigger than a city, yet just right for this small town.

"Hard at work or hardly working?" I said, hoping they hadn't heard that line in the last five minutes.

"Yard clerk to the shingles!" bellowed Ron Spitballer on nine walkie-talkie radios. "Right now, or you're all fired!"

"We ain't getting anyone anything," said Mustache, turning off his walkie-talkie just as Ron threatened to slash all their vehicle tires. All the other workers nodded. "It's like building our own coffin. Yeah. The longer it takes for this stuff to get out of the yard, the longer we'll have a job."

"What are you guys going to do?" I asked. "Work at Ramona?"

Nine spits hit the ground at the same time. Followed by nine shouts of "NEVER!" Followed by nine curses of varying degrees of incivility. Followed by one, "Yeah."

"Might have to leave," said Mustache. "Might have to try Big*fart*. Might have to move in with Mom and Dad. Might have to be a cat herder. Might have to do something. Yeah. Oh yeah."

"You guys going to the thing tonight?" I asked. "The mayor's thing?"

"What's the point? It's all lost," said Hot Rob, one of the younger workers.

"What if we all did something?" I said, not at all sure what *something* meant.

"You're young, Joey. Yeah," said Mustache. "Life don't work like that. Nope. Yeah. But if you lead the way, I'll be right behind you." He laughed like the sound of a trumpet caught in a hurricane.

"Well..." I paused. Why was I getting emotional? I wasn't going anywhere. My dad's job was safe. What did it matter to me? What did it matter to my future?

"Well, yeah," said Mustache.

"Well," I said, nodding my head.

I biked away—the wind at my back. I was going back home. And leaving home.

Chapter Fourteen

A Town Scattered

"Take the older kids if you want; the younger ones are going to bed."

A whine from Rebecca and Sam ensued, followed by a cry from Lyda. Mom's law *is* law. They weren't going.

"We'll take the truck, then," said Dad. Any excuse to take the old orange truck was fine by him.

The wind was dying, the evening sun lowering to the west. A sprinkle of rain fell while Johnny, Josh, Ellie, and I rode alongside Dad. We were squished into the truck like sardines. There were no backseats. Three times, Dad stopped and had me dry off the windshield with an old squeegee that Danny, the award-winning gas station attendant, once gave us. The old orange truck's wipers hadn't worked in my lifetime. Probably not in Dad's lifetime as well. Finally, my dad got sick of pulling over to clean the windshield and leaned out the side window with the squeegee whenever necessary. It was probably illegal. "Rules are meant to be broken," my dad would say whenever it was to his advantage.

The rain drifted away when we entered town. We joined the parade of vehicles dutifully coming to the "mayor's thing" and wound our way toward the main street. The parade didn't last long. We parked far back instead and started walking. There were cars and people everywhere. Saskariver was alive again. For one last time, I imagined.

Walking towards that dreaded main street—I'd come to hate being there as it was—the sound of live music met our ears. Some local band called Craven Arrest was playing their only four songs on repeat. I distinctly remember that the drummer was pretty good. For a second or two, I thought he resembled Danny, the award-winning gas station attendant. He seemed a little mysterious with sunglasses and a hood over his head. But that's impossible. One person couldn't have *that* much talent. Right?

Helium-filled balloons were being handed out. Children ran around with painted faces and sugar-heavy treats. Several television station reporters were on hand for the festivities. They looked nervous. Like a killer moose was waiting to pop out of the shadows and eat them all. Meanwhile, a few activities were set up, including a basketball free-throw challenge. My dad asked if any of us wanted to try. He said he'd pay. I told him we'd go broke if I tried.

Next to the rock band was a stage constructed using the flatbed from a semi-truck trailer. Large twinkle lights were strung around it for a charming, hopeful ambiance. A cake, the biggest I'd ever seen, was sitting on a table on the stage. It was going to be an emotional night. The cake was in tiers.

"Well," said Dad. "It's eight o'clock now. They'd better get started."

As though they were waiting for those words from Dad, the band stopped playing, and smooth-talking Stormin'

Lorne Redvers from the local radio station walked onto the stage. The entire town of Saskariver—what was left of Saskariver—crowded around the stage.

"Okaaaaay!" said Lorne, his microphone squealing with feedback. "Soooo. We're going to get started there. Okaaaaay. First of all, thank you all for coming out tonight there. And thanks to tonight's sponsor, Ramona Lumber Store. Be sure to get some of them there lumber and nails and stuff from them tomorrow."

Only one person clapped. It was Mayor Nutrine standing at the foot of the stage.

"Okaaaaay! Sooooo. If yer like me, you're probably wondering why you're here. Besides the great music. Check out Crave-a-Respiratory on my radio station there, Hailstorm FM. The best radio station in the Northeast. Okaaaaaay."

My dad looked at his watch. "Quarter after eight now," he said, "they'd better get started."

Again, these words were the blessing needed to move the evening along.

"Okaaaaaay! It's time to announce our honored guest. She's no stranger to all of us. A large woman in our lives. Er, large figure. Persona. She's got a large, er, big stuff to say to us about the future of Saskariver. Okaaaaaay. Please give a welcome to large Mayor Nutrients!"

This time, there were no claps. Craven Arrest cut into a quick thirty-second music solo while Mayor Nutrine climbed up the stage. Man, that drummer was good! Maybe it was Danny?

Mayor Nutrine took the microphone from Lorne Redvers. She cleared her throat, smiled—which wasn't a pleasant sight—and pulled out a speech from the top pocket of her red pantsuit.

"Thank you, Lorne. Thank you, Craving Aroasting. And thank you all for coming out tonight. Tonight, I'm calling it Saskariver's birthday!"

The sky was darkening. The atmosphere was ominous. From behind the stage, I could make out a crew of town workers setting up various fireworks and other eruptive devices. I'm not sure setting off loud explosives at the very site of the original town explosion was going to heal anyone's trauma.

"It's a new beginning. Today is the day we move past our town's explosion and into an explosive new future!"

She looked at the drummer. I think he was supposed to do a *ba-dum-ching* with his drums. He didn't even flinch, though. What a drummer. I'd vote for him.

"Saskariver is a diamond in the rough," she began. "Literally, we are a diamond of a place." She paused, savoring the moment. "What I mean to say is, the explosion has brought much good."

Mayor Nutrine reached into another pocket in her red pantsuit outfit and pulled out a small shiny object. It was a diamond. *My* diamond. It had been removed from its kimberlite home, and now shone in perfect brilliance. I bit down hard on my molars.

"I have personally found the key to our future." She held up the diamond. "This is a diamond! I recovered it from right here. Right at the site of the explosion! We've since drilled down, and I can confirm that downtown Saskariver is built right on a massive diamond reserve site! We're rich!"

Craven Arrest kicked into another thirty-second solo while the crowd murmured in shock, awe, and confusion. When the buzz settled down, the mayor continued.

"I have already communicated with the necessary government officials and other large businesses, such as the Ramona Lumber Store head office in New York. I can tell you that this diamond find will save us! We will start clearing out downtown completely. All buildings within three hundred yards from here will be moved or taken down. The owners will be paid far more than their buildings are worth. That's right! From here down to that church over there. We're making room for progress! We're making room for the future! And we're starting at seven a.m. tomorrow!"

A slight cough was heard at the back of the crowd. A sniffle from the middle of the pack. And a gasp from the front. Otherwise, it was complete silence.

I looked around uncomfortably. Jaws dropped. Eyes bulged from sockets. Drool spilled to the ground. People were stunned, but nobody said anything.

I thought of this town. I thought of the people. I thought of the places. The Ron Spitballers. The Green Truck Driver, gym teachers, and Lumber Coop workers. I thought of the churches, chicken balls, pools, and gas stations. I thought of what it was and what it was to become. And I didn't like it.

Who was I to say anything? I was an unknown. A nothing. A misfit in a town of misfits. Looking around the stunned crowd, it occurred to me: If something out of the ordinary needs to happen, maybe it should be from someone out of the ordinary.

"I... I don't know," I said. Quietly, yet loud enough to get the attention of those around me. I tried again. "I don't know if that's good."

This time, Mayor Nutrine noted that I said something. I don't think she knew what it was, thankfully. For what happened next never would've been possible had she known.

"You! Oh boy! Come up on stage! I want to tell the town you had a hand in this!"

Oh boy is right. This was it. I looked at my dad. He nodded, and I walked towards the stage. I was shaking so much, I'm sure if I were to take a shower, the water would've missed me.

"What's your name, honey?" asked the mayor.

Turning to look at the entire town, I muttered, "Uh, Joey. Joey Storthoaks."

"Well now, Joey Storthoaks! You had a hand in making this happen. This is your responsibility! You helped me find the diamond. You must be proud."

"Not you, Joey! You couldn't have done this!" I heard from the crowd. It was the familiar voice that sounded like a trumpet.

"Joey did this?" It was the voice of Mr. Garzy, the bee-keeper.

"Joey?" rang Evelyn Carnduff's unmistakable voice.

More murmuring ran through the crowd. I was a traitor. Taking a breath, I politely took the microphone from the mayor's hand, took another breath, and said what I needed to say.

"Thank you, Mayor Nutrine. Uh..." Deep breath. Just do it. God help us all. "I found the diamond, but I didn't know it would lead to this. If I did, I never would have handed it in."

The mayor's face dropped in shock. So, I raced ahead with my words.

"This blasted town is worth more than any diamond, or diamond mine for that matter. What's the point of making money and losing your home? Losing your life! Who you are! If you ask me, we should be rebuilding what we have..."

She pulled the microphone from my hand while yelling for security. Lorne Redvers came running onto the stage. Shouts started penetrating from all four corners of the crowd.

"Grab him, Lorne!" said the mayor. Unfortunately, she said this right into the microphone. This riled up people even more. Sensing the change, I did something foolish. Something to get attention. Something because I said someone had to do *something*.

I bobbed around Lorne and ran towards the cake. It was twice my size. The table holding it was hardly able to withstand its weight. Lorne chased me around to the left; I ducked right. He chased me to the right; I ducked left. Meanwhile, Mayor Nutrine shouted vile threats that I should be caught and tied to a firework. We were the Three Stooges comedy act performing in front of all of Saskariver. All that was lacking was for me to say a few, "Nyuk, nyuk, nyuks."

After a dozen loops around the table, Lorne was getting tired. He bent down to catch his breath. His timing couldn't have been better. Mayor Nutrine was now stomping over to get me. She didn't see Lorne and went tipping over him, a complete somersault, and landed heavily in front of the cake. Using all my strength, I lifted my side of the table. The cake started sliding the other way. The slide became an unstoppable torrent of wheat and plastic-flavored icing. The cake went plummeting down onto the mayor. It covered her from head to heel. I could hear her scream and roar as she tried to get up. The cake, mayor, and dignity of the town went sliding off the stage and crashed hard on the ground below.

The splatter of cake and mayor-parts thundered. For some reason, the men managing the fireworks took it as a signal to let the show begin. Crashes and screams rang through the late evening. Fireworks lit up the sky. It was almost perfect chaos.

Of all things, Marty the Moose came charging in. What a celebrity. The television reporters cried in terror, screaming to get out or die. Marty ignored their vile shouts and ran straight for the cake, making his trademark smile to the crowd before dipping into a large mouthful of his favorite food. He snagged a piece of the mayor's ear in the process and pulled hard. She screamed loud enough to wake the dead. This spooked Marty, and he ran straight into the fireworks display. Poor Marty knocked over several rows of set-up explosives, sending bombs of color and destruction sailing in all directions. People hit the floor, covering their heads, crying, cursing, praying. Others ran in circles, bumping into each other, getting up and running more circles. Now, it *was* perfect chaos.

I had to get out and fast. The stage was not a safe place to be. Jumping over Lorne, I bounded off the stage and ran—ran for my life. I ran past the band, through the last of the crowd, and down the street. Fireworks ushered me forward. And I ran some more. Through the street, past the church, and still another firework spooked me into running further. Into the cemetery, past graves of the souls seeking eternal rest, and into the dark. I ran for my life. I ran for my freedom. I ran for the sake of running. I ran because I did not know how to stop.

I ran until I hit a tombstone that had reached out and tripped me. I tumbled over, knocked a loose piece of plywood, and crashed down a complete six feet into an unfilled grave. My left arm hit hard as I fell. Not this again. How many times can an eleven-year-old tumble into a grave?

And that's why I'm sitting here, in the present, at the bottom of this grave.

I don't want to get out, even if I could.

CHAPTER FIFTEEN

GRAVE CIRCUMSTANCES

I t's me. In the present. Talking to you right here and now. In a grave. I am alive and, I suppose, thankful to be alive. Jesus didn't come to get me. I'm not right with Jesus.

I messed things up too much. It's dark and gloomy, cold and miserable. I feel depressed. Being depressed makes me disappointed with myself. This, in turn, makes me upset, which leads to feeling depressed—a vicious cycle. I am hidden from the world, *inside* the world, and maybe it's better this way. Oh Joey, you sure made a mess of things this time.

I should be shouting for help. But I can't. I suppose I need to stay alive. And I can't get the attention of the river man, the one who kills his victims and feeds them to the mountain lions and wolves. To stay alive is to stay quiet. I remain with my thoughts.

Mostly, I am thinking about myself. Self-centered, I know. I am thinking about how hard it is to belong. To want to be with others, strike up a conversation, and be considered normal. But then I pull away, go off alone, and people think I'm rude. Over time, I've grown hard to what they think about me. This leads me to stay on my own even more.

It's getting late. I'm sorry, Mom and Dad. You must be sick with worry. I'm alright. I'm sorry for the trouble. I wish I could make it up.

I'm thirsty. My lips are cracking. My head is starting to swoon. I'm just going to lay down a little. It sure is cold down here.

I'm sorry, Clay. I don't understand why you pick on me. Or maybe I don't want to understand. But I shouldn't have stolen your clothes at the pool.

I'm sorry, Evelyn. You're a good girl. Insofar as a girl can be good. I get embarrassed so easily. I shouldn't have tried to mess with you by acting like a weird know-it-all.

I'm just going to lay my head on my arms a bit. Why are tears falling on my cheeks? I don't want to cry. The harder I try not to, the more tears come. I don't matter. I've only let others down. I've been given what I deserve.

A grave. I'm falling asleep in a grave. Maybe I'm dying. Can I ever rise? I don't know how to. How can I rise up from this grave? Will someone save me?

I'm cold.

I'm lonely.

I don't belong.

How?

I've never been so miserable. That's what being alone with my thoughts has brought me after all these years.

It's all my fault.

A crack of light penetrates the morning sky. It has filled my grave ever so gently. I slept. Slept hard. On hard earth. In hard earth. And now I must get to my feet. I must stretch and breathe deeply in this life. I have been given another day. Another chance. Saved. I feel like roaring. I am new. In my own small, insignificant way, I have risen.

"Yes!" I say out loud. My enthusiasm just carried me away! I pause, scared to take a breath. I might be awake, but I can't wake up *him*.

I hear a rustling noise. No, it's definitely a walking noise. It's coming closer. I haven't taken a breath in a minute or more. He's coming. I know it.

Now, there's a hint of a shadow coming down. Just a hint. The shadow of death. *I walk in the shadow of death.* I fear all evil.

"Well, what the... A talking grave?" comes a gruff voice.

A face bends over. I can't make out who it is. It's a silhouette. But he can make out who I am. A light shines from a flashlight. It blinds my eyes. I blink and cover my eyes. I can't see.

"I know you, kid," he says. "I've seen you before."

I'm busted. I have been here before. I disturbed his...home.

"You're coming up," he says. It is an order not to be disobeyed.

The light goes off, and a shadowy arm reaches down. I'm supposed to grab onto it. Grab onto it, be pulled up, and then get gruesomely killed. I hesitate. Come on, Joey. Rise. Rise, then run.

I grab the hand. The grip is firm. Immediately, another hand reaches out and takes hold of me. Two hands pull.

I kick at the side wall of dirt. I kick and pull and fight my way up. I need to get up and get out.

My foot strikes the grass. I am out. I am free. Without looking, I turn and run. Dizzy and confused, I flee.

"Hey now!" he says. "Get back here!"

Not a chance; I stumble and run, run and stumble. I run until I'm out of breath, which is surprisingly not very far this morning. I slow down and peek over my shoulder. I see the man. The stranger. The terror. My heart jumps. I know who he is.

* 🫎 *

"Come back!" says the man. "You look awful."

I consider the wisdom of his words, that I do feel faint, and that I could use some help. More than that, I judge this man to be...trustworthy?

I walk towards him, careful not to trip on another tombstone. Tombstones are deadly. I note how the morning is fast approaching now. Robins are singing. Chickadees are calling. It is a wondrous thing how the world returns each morning. With hope. With joy. I'd have given up on humans long ago if I were the world.

"Come get some water at least, eh?" he says. His face is unshaven with white stubble. He's wearing an old-styled tan jacket. Poofy, dated, but warm. He takes off his jacket and comes to put it around me. But first, he pulls a pair of work gloves from a pocket and then puts them on his hands. His gloves, more than his face, remind me who he is. He is the man from church. The one who comes every

Sunday. The one who said last Sunday we needed more faith. The one whose name I don't even know.

Embarrassed by my attempt to flee, I build a bridge and get over myself. I decide to introduce who I am. "I'm Joey. I fell in last night trying to get away from the fireworks!"

He laughs. "I'll bet! It was quite a show. The town went crazy! Those reporters will never be back now!"

"You saw it?" I ask.

"Yeah. From a distance."

Finally, I take the plunge. "I see you sometimes from a distance, like at church. But you're *never* really around others. I mean…who are you?"

"Paul. Lived here my whole life, Joey." His voice has a soothing rasp to it. "I like people, don't worry. I like being on my own, too, though. It's hard to explain."

"I know what you mean."

"I'm not sure you do. Not entirely."

He leads me back to his living quarters. There is a blue tarp. A few cooking items. A makeshift hut of sticks and spruce boughs. It's primitive. Shocking. But it suits Paul just fine.

He takes out a bottle of water and hands it to me. The water is cold and doesn't feel great going down. I'm thirsty but not ready to drink icy liquid in abundance. Recovery from my dizziness might be harder than I first expected.

"You hungry?" he asks.

I'm thinking about food the way I do while daydreaming at church. Which is to say, I'm starving. And I think food is just what I need. I don't want to take his food. I want to go home. There's food there. Besides, he looks like he might not have much. So, I say I'm fine. He shakes his head and says he's got lots of food—a never-ending abundance. I don't want to be rude. Or at least seem rude. I say a bit of food would be fine. I need to eat. My head gets dizzy so quickly.

"Let's go get some," Paul says, and turns towards a trail.

"Where are you—" I start.

"Down to the river," he interrupts. "We'll catch our breakfast easy when it's this early."

I am amazed, and even forget to run down to the police station to report myself. It's early anyway, I reason. Just a quick touch of food would be fine. My head hurts too much now, anyway.

We move down his steep trail through trees and bush until the river is in sight. The path almost does me in, and I need to pause at the bottom to stop my head from spinning. Paul hands me an old fishing pole. It has a rusty hook on it. He takes another pole and bends over to the ground. He scratches at the dirt and weeds until he finds what he's looking for. He picks up two worms, hands one to me, and then baits his hook. Without a word, he starts casting.

I bait my hook and follow suit. I think my chickens at home would go crazy for that worm. I'll bet someone could catch chickens with a fishing rod.

Soon, Paul and I are staring ahead at the free-flowing Saskatchewan River. Shoulder to shoulder. The water is gentle, though a hidden power lurks within. It moves where it wills, unconcerned about the world around it. It is a force. A loner. A piece of beauty. I can relate. Paul, I think, can relate.

I decide I need to make the conversation happen. Practice my social skills, as Mom might say. It's a pivotal moment. Could you not blow it, Joey?

"Do you like cats?" I ask. I just blew it.

"Huh?" he says.

"Just nothing..." My voice sounds weak.

"I've got a cat. Protects my stuff. In case youngsters try to crash my place. He's not here right now. Must be avoiding you."

I had forgotten, but Paul remembered. His cat scared the life out of me once, and I probably scared a few lives out of it.

"You go to my church, don't you?" I ask Paul, changing the subject.

He grunts. I look ahead at the water. A jump comes from close to the other side. A pelican swoops after it. Some call pelicans ugly. I think they're majestic. The tremendous bird rises again, empty.

"Been going there for years and years," he says.

"How come we never see you at church events or even town events?" I ask. Was that a polite thing to ask?

Paul's eyes shrink. He sounds like the question hurts him. "I guess I've lived my life in such a way it's hard to go back. It's hard to change."

"You could come back! That'd be great."

I didn't mean much by my words. It's just an honest little answer from an eleven-year-old. It surprises me when Paul sniffles—just a little. I think what I said touched him.

"That'd be something. I'm maybe a little too... I don't think I could belong much anymore. Too old. You know.

And people tell crazy stories in a small town. It's hard to belong at this point."

"At a church?" I say. "Or in town?"

"Yeah."

"You know, I'm the same way." My eyes squint uncomfortably, but my words flow with ease. "Right now, I'm supposed to be home. But I'm here. And I'm scared to go back. Not just that I'll get in trouble. I'm scared I made a show of myself in front of the entire town. I wrecked things pretty good."

"I'll get you home soon."

"Thanks."

Paul looks uneasy. He's struggling with something.

I speak up. If an eleven-year-old can't be bold, then no one can. "So why are you living here?"

Paul grunts. He looks down the river. He shakes his head. Finally, he speaks. "I..."

He pauses. Coughs. Grunts again. Then continues.

"I used to have a family. Years ago. A wife. A son. There was a crash. No one's fault. An icy road. And just like that, I lost my wife and son. It was years ago, though. I still have big scars on my hands from where the windshield hit me."

I am stunned. I mutter a useless but heartfelt, "I'm sorry."

"It was years ago. Being out here helps me heal. I think. But what hasn't helped is that my own family felt ashamed of what happened. I mean my sister. Like the crash caused her embarrassment. She's gone her own way. I've drifted away to mine. I struggled to keep down a job after. I lost my house. More like I abandoned it. And here I am. Alone. Disowned. Like some kind of..."

"Misfit?" I say.

Before Paul can answer, he starts reeling in. Soon, a two-pound walleye is flopping on the sandy shore—a perfect breakfast. Paul takes the fish, ends its life, and proceeds to fillet it with a knife tucked in the nearby bushes. As he does so, he takes up the conversation again.

"I saw you last night. You were quite brave. You think you're nothing like me. But you were the only one who did something. That's more than I, or anyone else, can say."

He starts deboning a fillet. I check my line to see if the worm is still there, then launch it into the deep.

"I'll tell you something, Joey. Can you keep it to yourself?"

"Sure."

"My last name's Nutrine. That's right. Same as the mayor. I'm her brother. She married. Never changed her last name. She's the mayor of this town. And I'm a bum living by the river."

"Wow."

"I just gave up on life. Or my life gave up on me. But I stopped fighting for things. That's what."

"It's never too late," I say. I just blurted it out, yet I think the words packed a punch once again.

Paul paused and thought for a long time. "Tell me something, Joey. How do you expect me to go back to a normal life? I'm an outsider. And I'd probably wreck my sister's career."

"Your sister's wrecking the town with her career," I stammer. Whoops.

He laughs. "Don't be ashamed. You're right! She's wrecked this town. She loves her fame and glory. She really loves her diamonds, too. She always did. Used to steal Mom's jewelry and wear it secretly. Then, one day, she lost an earring. Blamed me. Said I sold it for money. Ah, what I mean is, it's best I leave her and stay as I am."

I'm puzzled. Grownups. Who can figure them out? My hazy mind wanders elsewhere while Paul lights a fire and throws fish fillets on a pan.

"Paul, you said that this town needed faith... Do you still think so?"

"Sure do," he says quickly. "This whole world does."

"What does that look like?"

"Oh, I don't know," he mumbles thoughtfully. "Maybe less worry. More trust. It's like...this river. Just floats on. Life takes you like that. Trust you're on the right path. Stay on the path. It'll take you where you need to go. People are always wanting to jump off course. One little trouble, and they're gone. An explosion, and they abandon their life."

"A crash, and they give up on life," I mutter quietly. Thankfully, Paul doesn't hear it.

The fish is ready. I'm hesitant to reel in my line. So, I snag a mouthful of fish. It's as fresh as can be. Juicy and sweet. My strength starts returning. So, too, my willingness to return home. As for faith, I think I start understanding what Paul is saying. Like this river. Get on. Trust. Stay on. In my heart, I whisper a prayer. One for Paul. One for me. One for my town.

With that, my line starts pulling. At first, I groan. I must've caught Saskatchewan, as my dad would say. But it tugs again, up and down.

"Well, now!" says Paul, his voice rising. "You've got yourself a fish!"

It's a battle, alright. It's a fish. A nice one. Too nice. I grunt and shake as I try reeling in the catch. The line drags right back out as soon as I make a few turns.

"You need help!" says Paul. I'm grateful for the offer. He takes the line and fights the fish. For endless minutes, he pulls and turns and pulls some more. After five minutes, Paul hands the rod to me, telling me he's tired, and so is the fish.

By now, I'm able to reel in the catch. The beast has stopped fighting. It's resigned itself to what will be. And I surprise myself by saying out loud, "Have faith!"

The fish rolls up to shore. Paul grabs the line and tugs it forward. It starts flopping. It's the biggest fish I've ever seen. The leviathan of walleye. The beast of the river. The fruits of faith.

"Joey!" Paul screams, jumping up and down. "Take *that*, Karen! Haha! Joey! Joey! Joey!"

I look down at the fish flopping on the shore. My hands are shaking. My whole body now, too. "Uh... We need to take this old boy to town!"

Chapter Sixteen

A Town to Save

"Paul, we both need to go back to town. Together."

"Young sir, it would be an honor," says Paul.

Paul rummages around in a stash of supplies tucked into the bush by the river. Soon, he pulls out an old bedsheet. Next, he does something unpleasant but necessary. He takes a rock and ends the fish—this beautiful creature. But now, it is part of a bigger cause. I don't flinch. I'm used to this type of thing. It's natural.

We wrap the fish in the bedsheet. Paul holds up one end over his shoulder; I take the other. We march forward. To the trail. Up the steep embankment. Through Paul's makeshift yard. Onward through the graveyard. It's quite the funeral procession for this slimy beast.

The fish is heavy. I know it's going to be a grind. I have some of my strength back, but not all of it. Gravity pulls hard on this fish. Like when I had to hold our twenty-pound cat Happy for an entire baseball game so he wouldn't run away. How the heck did *that* cat ever sneak into our vehicle?

We start walking into town. It must be after seven in the morning. The town rises early, and people will be out and about. I suggest to Paul that we come through the back road. I tell him I have a plan. He grunts his displeasure but agrees.

We walk past the Lumber Coop. Mustache and a few of the boys are heading in for one of their last days of work.

"What you got there? A dead body? Looks fishy. Yeah," says Mustache.

"Sure do!" I say.

"Not Little Mustache!" he cries in fear as I set to unfold the bedsheet.

"Holy mackerel!" shouts Hot Rob.

"Walleye," I correct him.

"Wow! Yeah. Where the heck are you going?" asks Mustache, taking in the strangeness of the situation.

"To the main street," I say. "You should stop by there soon."

He smiles. "Yeah. Oh yeah."

"Oh yeah," I reply.

Paul and I carry the fish onward. Past the road heading to the museum. Past Ramona. I swear the road to that building is paved with diamonds. Past the mechanic's shop. Green Truck Guy pulls up behind us. He starts following us, a fitting escort.

We have a parade now. I have something much better than coupons for ten percent off apples. Past the Chinese restaurant. Past the police station. At this point, I stop.

A policeman stands out front. He comes running over. "You're that boy! We've been looking all over for you!"

"I'm fine!" I yell. "I'm just fine! Call my parents right away! Tell them to come downtown!"

"I can't do that!" says the officer, but I've already turned towards my intended path. A police vehicle pulls out to follow with lights flashing but gets stuck in the parade's traffic.

We take a turn to make this trek longer. We need a bigger parade. Past the empty swimming pool. Past the post office. The old men are back, staring at Paul and me and our mysterious package.

"Thanks, guys!" I shout at them. They probably have no idea why I said that.

"Did he say *dance prize*?" says one of them.

"Eh? *Pants pies*?"

A real crowd is gathering now. We are approaching the main street, where my world was ending just hours ago. Our main street is deserted. But there is trouble brewing farther ahead, near where I should have come first with the fish. At least now I have a crowd to witness what must be done.

It's not looking good. There are three excavators fired up and ready for business. Not our local Chumpa company's diggers, either. These were shipped in from elsewhere. I see a lineup of six dump trucks, too. A crew of men are standing around in safety vests and hard hats. It has begun.

The arm of one excavator extends forward, straight into the roof of a green house with a charming front awning. The house folds like a deck of cards. The machine's bucket grabs at boards, windows, and all the other blood and guts of the home. It also removes its heart and soul, tossing it into a dump truck like yesterday's newspaper.

Another excavator cranks its way towards the next house on the block. A blue house with white trim. It is in the way and must be taken down. There are diamond mines to create, dreams to fulfill, lives to destroy. I knew a kid who lived in this house with his family. That was long ago. Where is the kid now? Not here, I hope.

Crash!

A home no more. But a future home to greed and success. The diamonds are calling, so it must go.

Paul and I still carry our surprise catch. It weighs heavily, resting on the shoulder. A cross I must carry. I look ahead and groan. The next excavator creaks towards a different building. The church. My church. Paul's church. *Our* church.

Outside the church, there is a heated discussion. The mayor is dressed in a yellow pantsuit outfit to match the color of her teeth. She's holding a megaphone while screaming, "Out of the way! I have official permits! You're done!"

So she's been working at this for a while. In the hiddenness of her own office. And now she's springing to action. Or trying to. Only one thing is in her way.

Standing, or rather kneeling, is Father Wally. Though alone, his face is firm, his faith strong. But stronger than Father Wally are the men from the excavating crew ready to remove him. I imagine he'll be escorted away, violently, soon.

My parade has arrived. There are more people than I could've imagined. Word gets out fast in Saskariver. Danny. Coach Macklin. Miss Fancy Spudd. Xander Humboldt. Bob Yorkton. Mrs. Pearl. The entire town has woken up. Even kids are awake and present. The smashing of houses will do that. There's Clay, Evelyn, and many others.

The place is ready for what must happen. I take a deep breath. It's almost my time to act.

"Get out, priest!" shouts the mayor. Her voice lowers when it is angry. Like a demon mumbling deep as it tumbles out of bed.

"Pray for those who persecute you," says Father Wally. His voice sounds strong when challenged.

"He's not going!" says the mayor. She is nearly delirious. "Carry him away! It's time for this old building to go! We have progress to build. Out of the way, priest!"

"Not today!" I shout, making my entry onto the scene.

"Paul!" shouts the mayor upon seeing her brother.

"Karen," Paul says.

"What are you doing here?" she says, then her lips crease upward. "You don't *belong* here."

"I belong as much as you do or anyone else," he replies.

"It's over. I'm through. This blasted town!"

Mayor Nutrine swirls her hand in a commanding motion, and an excavator lunges forward. Its bucket raises over Father Wally. Over Paul and me, and grasps at the church's front stained-glass window. This is about to be the end.

"Not *my* blasted town!" I shout. "No!"

"Yeah," comes a reply.

Barrelling at full throttle comes Mustache, driving his Lumber Coop forklift like a bat out of...

"Hello! Yeah," he calls, driving his forklift in between the excavator and the church. The excavator stops its forward motion. The driver is flustered.

The forklift's forks are raised to the eye level of the excavator's driver. The driver weaves his head left and right, trying to see ahead of him. Mustache keeps the forks up to block the driver's vision. Now is my chance.

"I have the answer to your prayers!" I shout above the crowd, above the roar of the excavator, above the squeals of the mayor.

With that, Paul and I unwrap the package. Together, we hold up our prize where the mayor, the crowd, and Father Wally can see.

"Ohh!" cries the crowd.

"Yeah. Oh yeah," trumpets Mustache.

"Joey!" says Evelyn.

"Mamma mia!" says Father Wally. "It's true! It's real. It's happening."

"I caught this fish this morning. From *our* river."

"So what?" yells the mayor.

Father Wally is already running to his truck to pull out his tackle box. He races back with a measuring tape and a scale.

"What's happening?" cries the mayor, oblivious to what it all means. "Get that smelly thing out of here!"

"Thirty-seven inches!" shouts Father Wally. A few seconds later, he adds, "And twenty-five pounds, seven ounces! That's got to be a new world record!"

The crowd goes ballistic.

"But so what?" screams the mayor.

Paul decides to explain. "Are you kidding? A world-record walleye. My dear sister, we are about to be flooded with fishermen from all over North America. Brace yourself. We're about to be saved."

"We are saved!" says Father Wally, holding up the fish. "This fish! This beautiful fish!" He kisses it.

The crowd rushes in. The mayor and her crew are squeezed out. Angry voices from the residents of Saskariver are heard.

"Get out of here!"

"I didn't even vote for you anyway."

"Danny for mayor!"

"We'll keep our church, thank you very much."

"We'll keep all of the town!"

"The fishermen coming will need sport equipment."

"And gas!"

"Chicken balls!"

"Gas from chicken balls!"

"I'll make her pay all her overdue library fines!"

With that, a town is awakened. A life rises from the grave. The seeds of restoration are planted in the fertile soil of people's minds. Made fertile by a fish and by faith.

I look at Paul. He's smiling. In his excitement, he starts talking to people. People he used to call friends, I imagine. His eyes are lit up. He, too, is feeling the seeds of restoration. Of rising.

"Joey!" calls my mom. She comes rushing in and hugs me. Dad joins in the hug. So, too, Sam and the others.

"Oh Joey!" she says, not even trying to fight back tears. "You...smell like fish!"

"Yeah, oh yeah," I say, smiling. "And now, so do you."

Chapter Seventeen

The End

"Who threw that potato?"

My dad is irate. All for one thrown potato. Never mind that the potato struck a chicken coop window, smashing it into tiny pieces.

I fess up. "I was trying to hit Ellie with it." As the words leave my mouth, I realize they were the wrong ones to say.

"You're lucky your fish taxidermy raised so much money," he huffs.

"Cause you're going to pay for a new window!" Secretly, I think he's very proud.

"Can we go get one now?" I ask.

He sighs. "Get in the truck."

We drive to town. Our town. We take our time getting where we need to go. We stop for gas. Danny, the award-winning gas station attendant, is there. He has an extra bounce in his step. A perfect rhythm to his motion. Like a drummer leading a band. He's happy. Happier than usual. So much so that he even offers to fix our windshield wiper—perfect worker that he is. Dad says no. Danny says yes. We settle on taking a new-used squeegee.

We stop to pick up a book from the library. Miss Fancy Spudd screams at me to be quiet when I say hello. But then she adds that she looks forward to my stories at the new library story hour, which will begin soon.

We join Green Truck Guy's parade. He is as slow as ever. And he never lacks followers anymore. His life is complete. The people behind him seem patient this morning. Like soaking in the hope of new life isn't the worst way to spend a Saturday.

We drive by Clay, and I wave. He waves back. He looks extra happy. Like not-moving-to-Bigfort happy. Maybe I'll see him at the pool again next summer. I shudder as images of tighty-whities flash in my mind.

We see Evelyn walking into the shoe store with her mom. I almost wave, but then I realize I'm driving with my dad. Awkward. But she sees us driving and waves first. I wave back gladly.

We drive by the post office, and I wave again. I feel like a king with all this waving. I then realize that no one is, in fact, standing outside the post office at that moment. Whoops. So what? I keep waving at the building.

We stop for a box of chicken balls. I pound back ten even before they have cooled off enough.

"Save some for your brothers and sisters," Dad warns.

"I'll buy some more for them instead," I answer, shoving another chicken ball in my mouth. Being half-rich has its perks.

We look out at the main street. Three new buildings are going up. A concrete truck and crew are currently pouring another foundation. I smile. It's more than just wood, concrete, metal, and windows. It's a feeling of renewal. A feeling of belonging. A feeling of being well.

We make our way to the final stop. As Dad shuts off the truck, I hear a sound. Soon, I am holding Little Mustache in my arms. He, or she, purrs. I carry Little Mustache while we walk to the main checkout counter.

"Another window," says Dad. He doesn't even need to give the size anymore. They know.

"Anything else?" asks Ron Spitballer. He looks relaxed for once. Relieved. Peaceful. In a miserable sort of way.

I point to a sign on a shelf. It says, *My Pets Make Me Breakfast*. "I'll buy that also. For the chicken coop."

Ron smiles. Everyone is happy. He picks up the walkie-talkie. "Any of you worthless and lazy yard clerks there? Get your fat guts to the window shed, or you're all fired!" He puts the walkie-talkie away, and says, "Have a great day." It is well with him.

We step out into the morning air. The weather is cooling. Summer is leaving. The Lumber Coop will stay busy throughout. There are businesses to rebuild. Lives to repair.

"I got your window! Yeah," says a familiar voice.

"Mustache!" I say. "How are things?"

"Little Mustache!" he cries, dropping the window.

There are pieces of glass everywhere. Mustache doesn't care. He takes the kitty in his arms and grins. "Guess I gotta get another window. Yeah. Busy as ever here. We're so busy that even the other people have to do some work!"

"Good! Just make sure you stock lots of these windows," says my dad.

"Oh yeah. Hey Joey! I heard the town was going to have a banquet for you! Yeah."

"No," I answer, "I decided I didn't want that. Too much, you know, well…"

"Oh yeah, always the same," laughs Mustache.

"Well," says Dad.

"Well," says Mustache.

"Well," I say.

And all is well.

ACKNOWLEDGMENTS

My wife and children: For the immense support and for always being there. Midlife crisis or not.

The small, insignificant places I've called home: Don't change (too much).

My editor, Shavonne Clarke: My writing has been described as: *A Bull in a China Shop.* Well, I say you are: *An Angel Sent from Heaven.*

Wendell Berry: For all the inspiration, tears, and laughs.

My launch team: Someone could write another *Hobbit,* and it still wouldn't go anywhere without a launch team. Such is the importance. Thanks for being the best!

All the students I've ever taught: For so much inspiration given. And, ahem, for buying so many of my books! Keep working hard and stay humble.

The Good Lord: Under the title: *Divine Infant of Prague.* All glory and praise.

A Mission for All

D id you know that Danny, the award-winning gas station attendant, used to be just a pretty good gas station attendant? So, too, his coworker Tyler. What happened?

One day, a customer came in. The customer was having a bad day. Tyler tried to be polite and cheer the customer up. When he did so, he dropped a bag of chips on the floor as he was bagging it. The customer frowned. On the way out, the customer told the boss how bad the service was and walked out. Tyler never really was the same afterward.

That same day, another customer came in. Danny tried to be friendly. But he, too, dropped a bag of chips on the floor while bagging it. Danny apologized. The customer laughed and said it was all good. Danny gave an extra-big smile to the customer. On the way out the door, the customer told the boss how wonderful the service was, and walked out. Danny never really was the same afterward. He had confidence and a bounce to his step. Soon, he developed into the award-winning gas station attendant we know today.

The point? As you "head out the door" from this novel, would you be willing to help me? To tell my "boss" you had a good visit? By that, I mean, could you please stop by Amazon and leave a positive review? And even let others know about this book? Like Danny, it would help me immensely. It would give me a bounce to my step and put a smile on my face.

I thank you sincerely, dear reader.

Who is Jennie?

I go for walks each night to reset my mind when I write stories. I walk down our street, past the elementary school, into an open field leading to the edge of town and into the endless prairie. If it's in the winter, I take my snowshoes. The sky is dark, and stars guide me as I go. I eventually stop my walk at the same location. It just so happens to be the local cemetery.

Yes, I stop at the cemetery...by the same random tombstone, in fact, and mutter a prayer that these souls might be welcomed into paradise. I then ask these same souls, if they're listening, to put in a good word for me with the Big Guy Upstairs. I specifically ask them to help me with my writing.

It's dark in a cemetery at night. Maybe it's even creepy. And I'm, I guess, talking to dead people in my mind. Please, just keep reading.

Writing novels is fun and personally rewarding. However, it has more than a few challenges. Off the top of my head, I can think of at least four thousand daily new challenges. Did you know something like four thousand new books are released on Amazon? Every. Single. Day.

Writing a story and getting it into the hands of readers is an indescribable challenge. It can be too much at times.

One day, I was feeling it. Feeling the pressure. Feeling the disappointment. Feeling what I suppose every author must go through. What was I doing? Wasting my time. Wasting my family's time. So, I went for a walk. I was done with writing. I was done with books. I was done.

It was daytime as I walked my familiar path. I'd never done this during the day. The sun shone as I walked towards the cemetery and stopped at my usual spot. I bowed my head and said my usual prayer. Looking up, searching for a Divine answer, I saw for the first time the gravestone I always stood beside. I read the name.

Jennie Book

Book?

Say whatever you want, but I felt it was a sign. A sign to make more books. With a pivot in focus, perhaps. But books nonetheless. And this is what I have done. I'm proud of them, too.

As for Jennie Book, she died in 1914 at the age of 25. Thank you, Jennie. I'll never forget you.

We walked inside. Then we groaned. This wasn't good.

It turns out that Sulphur Mountain has four peaks. The red chairs were all the way at the fourth peak. To get there involved real-deal mountain climbing. Like mountain climbing for experts. Lest you end up as poor Philip Stanley Abbott at Mount Lefroy in 1896. Tumbling down like a rag doll. Not pleasant.

"So," stammered Mom, "how are families supposed to get to the red chairs from here? Are they trying to kill us? Is that what this is about?" Her voice was escalating.

"No, not exactly," said Dad. "Just kill our wallets. Look over there. By the big windows. That's a rental place."

"What do you rent?" I asked. "Red chairs?"

"I wish," said Dad. "You rent mountain guides. I mean, you pay for someone to guide you along the mountain's ridge. And you pay to use all the safety equipment, helmets, and harnesses. I'll bet you pay per person. Hundreds of dollars per person."

"I don't like this," said Mom.

"Well, is this it?" I shouted. "We're done? After getting to six chairs!"

"It would be in the thousands of dollars, Joey," said Dad. I could see he was shocked and disappointed.

I stormed outside the interpretive center and walked down the path for a minute. The sky was clear, and the view was stunning. Banff was something. Imagine building a town in the most outstanding place you could find in the Rockies. The founding of the town of Banff was something like that. What did it matter? I'd always remember Banff as the place where my dreams were shattered.

I must've been grimacing as I stood looking down on the town because an older couple strolling past stopped to say something.

"You groovy?" asked the man. He had a massive head of gray dreadlocks, a tie-dye shirt, and baggy orange shorts. I'd say he was a hippy if I didn't know any better—an honest-to-goodness hippy. I'd never seen one before in Saskariver.

"I'm good," I lied.

"Forest," said an old lady in a hemp hat, long white dress, and rainbow necklace, "I think he's just chilling."

The man, apparently named Forest, nodded. "Got it, Chick," he replied.

"I'm just frustrated," I said. Of all the people to open up to... An old hippy couple at the top of a mountain! "We have one last red chair to get. One more! And it's way over on the last ridge. We can't afford to hire someone to take us there."

"Just like the government, man," said Forest. "Gotta crush the little dude."

"Something like that," I said before adding a "dude."

"You know, young wilderness man, life is like a journey," said Chick. "It's not about the destination. It's all the journey. And our journey should be love."

I didn't know what she was saying. Isn't life a journey *to* a destination?

"There's a saying I really dig," interrupted Forest. "There is freedom waiting for you in the breezes of the sky, and you ask, 'What if I fall?' Oh, but my darling, 'What if you fly?'"

"You mean I can fly to those red chairs?" I asked.

"You can do whatever your heart sets itself on," said Chick, showing her yellow teeth, or what was left of them, as she smiled.

"Uh, I need to go find my parents," I said.

"Look, son," said Forest. "Chill. I've been high up here many times, er, and I know how to fly to the fourth peak. Everyone goes on the top ridge or to the left of it. Nah. Dip a little below the ridge. On the right side. Just like, bypass the other summits. They'll distract you, man. Oh, and there's one psychedelic section. It's bad, dude. You got a ladder to success, though! Then you're like there. Copacetic?"

"I don't take things from strangers," I said.

"No, little dude!" laughed Forest. "Like, sound good?"

"Yeah, I think so."

"Then go fly!" said Chick. "Fly, little white dove, fly!"

"Maybe I will," I said, gathering my strength. "Maybe I will!"

I walked back to the interpretive center. How was I supposed to explain this to my parents? I decided to try something unusual. Something risky. Something unexpected. I was going to tell them the truth.

"Mom! Dad!" I shouted when I saw them standing inside the building. "I just met some old hippies! They said to go a little down from the ridge and to the right. Ignore the other summits, they said. And not to wonder about falling, but flying..." This was not panning out so well. "Like, flying like a white dove. Up high. We, er, can do it if it's a journey of love, er, and not a destiny. Our ladder of success..."

"Joey, are you okay?" asked Mom, concerned. I couldn't answer.

"I think he's trying to say that there is a better way to get to the fourth peak if we go to the right and a little down from the ridge and bypass the other peaks. Right?" said Dad.

"Copa...stetic? Copacetic?" I said.

Dad looked at Mom. She nodded. I smiled.

"Let's at least check it out," said Dad. "We'll go slow and safe. No falling."

"Only flying, dude," I said.

Also at Amazon:

ABOUT THE AUTHOR

D aniel J. Millette is a husband, father, writer, and educator living in North East Saskatchewan. Millette has a love for meaningful storytelling, as well as for mountain adventures with his family.

Please *subscribe/like* at YouTube, Facebook, Substack, or all three.

🍁 🫎 🍁

"If most of us valued food and cheer and song above hoarded gold, it would be a merrier world."

J.R.R. Tolkien, *The Hobbit*

www.ingramcontent.com/pod-product-compliance
Lightning Source LLC
La Vergne TN
LVHW041222080426
835508LV00011B/1036